TRADING WITH THE ODDS

USING THE POWER OF PROBABILITY TO PROFIT IN THE FUTURES MARKET

TRADING WITH THE ODDS

USING THE POWER OF
PROBABILITY TO
PROFIT IN THE
FUTURES MARKET

CYNTHIA A. KASE

IRWIN
Professional Publishing

Chicago • Bogotá • Boston • Buenos Aires • Caracas
London • Madrid • Mexico City • Sydney • Toronto

Times Mirror
Higher Education

ISBN: 1-55738-911-X

Printed in the United States of America
1 2 3 4 5 6 7 8 9 0 BS 2 1 0 9 8 7 6 5

FOREWORD

Several years ago I had the pleasure of taking Cynthia Kase on a speaking (teaching) tour to Italy and throughout many mid-eastern countries. I could easily discern that her mind was always at work. She would not take the traditional, commonly used technical analysis studies for granted, but would investigate carefully where others had blazed a trail, using their observations as a jumping off place from which to begin truly unique research.

An outside observer could see at the time that she had already mined the rough gems. I can tell it took work and dedication to polish these ideas into the methodology described in this book.

The book is filled with unique observations. They are best summed up by Cynthia's own comments on the present "state of the art" of the common routines published and used by technicians today. She feels that today, even with the availability of powerful computers, we are still living too close to the past where most technical analysis was done by hand, or, at best, using spreadsheets on fairly crude computers. Cynthia believes that we must make today's powerful computers WORK and work hard. With the increase in versatility of today's PCs, they are now capable of NEWER types of analysis if we tell them where to look.

I could easily cite many new ideas illustrated in this book, but I will choose just one and, for brevity, I will greatly simplify the concept. A trader who trades in two time frames traditionally uses the longer (weekly) chart and its signals to confirm the shorter (daily) chart. The trader's recurring dilemma is that he or she must wait for Friday's close to get the weekly confirmation. The trader would like to get his/her signals earlier, but the system specified requires a weekly confirmation. Cynthia asks why a week must end on a specific day. By using a "rolling" week for the last five trading days and their cumulative signal as the confirmation in building the system, both the daily chart and the weekly rolling chart can be evaluated EACH day. This example demonstrates Cynthia's dimensional expansion of a particular technique—breaking the traditional mold and looking for the trading edge.

To sum up, at this time I feel Cynthia's present work and the research evidenced in this book represents a new view of techniques.

If computer users or experienced technicians are looking for a trading edge, then this book, with its new look at technical analysis, is
one they will want to study and execute or make part of their trading
plan(s). Ms. Kase has found the gems and polished them, and leaves
the reader to put them in their setting.

Timothy C. Slater
Managing Director
Telerate Seminars

CONTENTS

FOREWORD V

INTRODUCTION XI

Chapter 1

**Increasing the Probability of
Success with Science and Statistics 1**

Replace Empirical Methods with Mathematically Derived Models 1

Manipulate Data to Improve Performance 1

Condense Information 1

Automatically Adaptive Indicators 2

Science, Not Magic 3

New Ideas Challenge Old Beliefs 3

Corporate Trading Must Be Accurate 4

While Never Easy, Trading Can at Least be Simple 6

Chapter 2

The True Nature of the Market 7

What is Important to Understand about the Market? 7

  The Market Is Symmetrical Across Time Frames 7

  Elliott's Wave Theory Is Essentially Correct 8

  Forecasting versus Trading 8

  The Market Is Mostly Predictable 9

  Market Extremes Are Unstable and Unpredictable 10

  The Logarithmic Spiral Describes Market Behavior 10

  There Is No Magic Formula or Easy Answer 11

Chapter 2 Appendix: Statistics Overview 12

Chapter 3

Developing a Strategy with Accurate Forecasting   20

Can People Really Forecast the Market Accurately?   20
The Six Kase Behavioral Laws of Forecasting   21
Market Geometry   25
Forecasting Methods   26
    Patterns and Rules   27
    The Math   29
    Corrective Move Retracements   30
    The Rule of Three   31
    Applying the Rules   31
      Shorter Than Rule   31
      Equal To Rule   33
      Longer Than Rule   34
      IT, IF, and IX Rules   35
      The Rule of Three   35
Retracements   35
The Forecasting Grid   38
    Forecasting Grid   38
    Forecasting Grid Legend   38
Chapter 3 Appendix: Using Chart Formations In Forecasting   40

Chapter 4

Improving the Probability of
Success with Time Diversification   48

Screening Trades   49
    Screening Using Trending Filters   50
    Screening Using Momentum Filters   53
    Bar Numbering Protocol   54
The Kase Permission Stochastic: Redefining Time   55
The Kase Permission Stochastic: A Better Screen   57
    Kase Permission Stochastic Filters   58
Condensing the Information   59
Kase Warning Signs   62
Scaling In Trades   63
Setting Up Charts   64
Scaling Up in Time Examples   65
    Trade One Example:
    Loss Minimized by Scaling Techniques   67
    Trade Two Example:
    Gain Maximized by Scaling Technique   67

Determining True Range   68
    Empirical Evidence that Price and Volume are
Fine-Tuning Entries   69
Price and Volume Proportional to the Square Root of Time   70
Chapter 4 Appendix: The Traditional Stochastic Indicator   72

Chapter 5

Increasing the Probability of Catching Market Turns   73

Why Traditional Momentum Indicators Cannot Be
Evaluated Statistically   74
What If We Could Define Overbought and Oversold?   75
The Solution: The Statistically Based Kase peakOscillator   77
PeakOscillator Works while Other Indicators Do Not   78
Improving Divergence Signals with the KaseCD (KCD)   83
Using the PeakOscillator in Trading   83
Stochastic Processes, Monte Carlo
Simulations, and Random Walk Mathematics   87
    Stochastic Processes   87
    Monte Carlo Simulations   88
The Kase Twist on the RW I   8 9

Chapter 6

Using Statistics to find Optimal Stop: Kase's Adaptive Dev-Stop   91

The Old Mousetrap: Stops Based on Fear   9 2
What Risk Does the Market Impose?   92
Stops Must Relate to the Market's Threshold of Uncertainty   93
The Wilder and Bookstaber Volatility Method   94
Variance of Volatility   95
The Skew of Volatility   96
Engineering a Better Stop: the Kase Dev-Stops   96
The Dev-Stop is as Close as Possible to the Best Balance   97
Charting the Dev-Stop   97
Using Candlestick Patterns to Accelerate Exits   97
Five Important Candlestick Patterns for Finessing Exits   98
Accelerating Exits Using Candlestick Patterns   101
    An Example of Accelerated Exits Using Candlestick Patterns   102
Using the Dev-Stop in Trading   103
Chapter Six Appendix: Gaps   1 0 6

Chapter 7

Walking Through Trades   111

Trade Plan for Example Trades   111
Timing Signals   112
    Monitor/Timing Chart, Exit Rules and Stops   113
    Daily Chart, Exit Rules and Stops   113
    Forecasting Rules   113
Walking through a Trade Using The Kase Rules and Indicators   114
    Example One: August 1995 Natural Gas   114
    Example Two: July 1995   126

Chapter 8

Freedom from Time and Space with Universal Bars   139

Rules for Formatting Equal Range Bars   140

References   145

Index   147

    Ordering Information   151

INTRODUCTION

"I can't believe that God plays dice with the universe."
Albert Einstein

My educational background was in engineering, while my trading background was as a corporate trader with a large oil company and then with a money center bank. Both these experiences have had a major impact on how I view the markets and how I trade. Accordingly, this book is about understanding the market from both an engineer's and a trader's points of view. It is about looking at the markets scientifically and accurately, without making the procedure for doing so too complex.

The book also offers views of the market from new perspectives. The reader will learn that simultaneously viewing the markets from multiple vantage points can provide profitable insights; that definitions and relationships based upon tradition are not necessarily the most accurate (15th-century mapmakers, for example, defined the world as flat); that an examination of statistically dependent and independent relationships can provide universal views of the market that are not impeded by differing units of measure in time or volume; and that, by combining statistics with common sense, aggressive stops can be placed with confidence and without fears of missed opportunities.

Where many older indicators are based strictly on empirical observations, we now have the tools to derive indicators from the natural structure of the market itself. Patterns that were difficult to observe with primitive tools now emerge for examination, and the reader is thereby led through complete and detailed step-by-step trades, utilizing his intellectual capacity and application of new tools to better understand the market.

Because I spent 10 years as a design and construction engineer and Naval Reserve engineering duty officer before I became a trader, I view the markets with an engineer's eye. Like pure research scientists, engineers think about the world in abstract mathematical terms. Unlike them, however, engineers are paid to convert their abstract mathematical understanding into practical applications. This book adopts the engineer's understanding of the market and applies practical and real-world terms, thus improving trading strategies and generating superior trading results.

Admittedly, this approach requires crunching lots of numbers quickly and accurately, an overwhelming obstacle in the past because the tools required for these calculations were extremely intimidating. The computational power of early computers was recognized, but getting at that power was tedious; computers were neither user-friendly nor affordable. Today, however, computerphobia is rapidly vanishing, and many people in the vast majority of developed nations are as familiar with their computers as they are with their microwave ovens and telephone answering machines. We have powerful, affordable, and user-friendly computers. I say, let's *use* them and make *them* work hard for us.

Once the reluctance to use new tools is overcome, all kinds of possibilities unfold. Markets can be explored in entirely new ways that can broaden our understanding by astronomical proportions. Those early mapmakers, for example, were exceedingly accurate in the things they could measure, but their perspective was limited to the use of the tools of their day. Consider the differences in their calculations and resultant maps if satellite imagery had been available to them.

One early technical indicator, developed in the late 1950s and early 1960s by Investment Educators, Inc., was the Stochastic, the most sophisticated tool extant. Though the Stochastic utilizes fairly rudimentary mathematical principles, calculating it by hand was still a tedious endeavor. During the ensuing 20 years, the programmable calculator, reverse polish notation (RPN) programming language, and the first affordable personal computer (PC) were developed. As these tools became available, traders took advantage of this increase in available computational speed, using it to perform many tasks.

In the late 1960s, Richard Donchian used the new calculators to test moving average systems (see Sidebar, "Moving Averages") and, in the early 1970s, published the results. In 1978, shortly after Hewlett Packard introduced RPN, Wells Wilder published a book called *New Concepts in Technical Trading*, which contained the directional movement indicator (DMI), parabolic indicator, relative strength index (RSI), and other indicators still popular today. (This book included steps for programming a calculator in RPN, making, for the first time, such sophistication available to the average trader.) In the late 1970s, Gerald Appel introduced the moving average convergence divergence indicator (MACD), which is derived from exponential moving averages, again adding a layer of mathematical complexity to calculations that would have been too time consuming to perform by hand.

These indicators became popular among technicians—and remain perennial favorites today—yet they viewed the market in terms of rudimentary, programmable calculators. No matter how insightful these early developers were about the market, they were still severely limited by the analytical tools available to them.

Surprisingly, while the computing capability of computer hardware has continued to develop at an astronomical rate, the development of early PCs seemed to mark the beginning of a period of stagnation in the development of technical analysis tools. In the early days of PCs, it was thought that no one would use more than 64K of RAM, but today most computer users feel hamstrung without many megabytes of RAM, and it is no longer necessary to make the mathematical compromises mandated by older technology, yet traders are still using methods developed for the calculator.

Once PCs had been developed with graphic capabilities, traders instantly recognized charting ramifications. Developing a graphic interface capable of synthesizing raw data from various exchanges and converting it into bar and line charts was a major undertaking, but the results were enormously popular with traders and opened the field to many new players. The effort required to program indicators on the original, hard-coded charting packages was great, but the payoff was considered to be worthwhile. In a total void, automatic calculation of a simple moving average, which would be displayed in relation to price data, along with a display on a computer screen, was a major advancement.

The reason technical analysis stalled at this point was that *modifying* the early computer code for existing indicators or modifying the graphic interface to include new indicators involved much time and expense. In an almost classic chicken-and-egg scenario, indicators had to be in great demand in order to justify the expense of reprogramming these early charting packages, but the indicators had to be widely available to traders (i.e., already programmed) in order to gain such popularity.

In the late 80s and early 90s, the front end graphic interfaces had finally been developed to the point at which they are customizable by the user, and traders can now create their own formulae and indicators in English and using standard mathematical notations. While the up-front effort is still considerable, there is no comparison to the hundreds of man-hours that the programming effort previously required. Traders now enjoy an increasingly greater ability to experiment with the concepts behind new indicators without waiting for a popular mandate.

As a trader, especially a corporate trader, with an inherent need for increased accuracy, and specifically directed to trade particular markets, and as an engineer, I have also explored and experimented with the market's inherent numerical relationships. In the process, I developed entirely new ways of understanding the markets that I turned into trading indicators which have proven to be extremely accurate and profitable. I am not concerned about the time required to perform calculations; once I theoretically determine that a concept should prove interesting, I program it into my PC and let the computer do the work for me.

Corporate traders are busy people. They are responsible for generating positive results without the benefits of diversification and with no choice as to which markets they will trade, using a conservative, highly accurate trading style. Corporate traders often have many other responsibilities and they operate under strict and particular mandates to make money under most market conditions while taking little risk.

This book is designed to explain these new state-of-the art indicators and techniques and to help traders use them for an increased understanding of the markets and to diminish risk and increase profits.

MOVING AVERAGES

The moving average is one of the simplest and most widely used indicators available for market analysis. The term moving average usually refers to a simple moving average of closing prices. It is calculated by choosing the length of the moving average one wishes to use (n bars), calculating the sum of the closing prices of those n bars, and dividing by n:

$$X = \frac{1}{n} \sum_{i=1}^{n} X_i$$

For example, to calculate an eight-day moving average, add the closing prices of the most recent eight days and divide by eight. (Note: Σ indicates summation, or sum all variables behind the term.) Standard summation notation is expressed as follows:

$$\sum_{k=1}^{n} a_k = a_1 + a_2 + a_3 + a_4 + \cdots + a_n$$

This expression is read as "the sum of a_k from $k = 1$ to $k = n$."

So the moving average equation reads: $X = 1/8$ (the sum of the closing prices of the eight days under consideration).

The most basic and traditional systems that interpret the market use a combination of a single moving average and closing price. In this type of system, closes above the moving average are assumed to indicate that the trend is up, and closes below the moving average indicate that the trend is down.

Many traders use a double moving average system, combining a "fast" moving average (for example, a nine-day moving average) and a "slow" moving average (for example, an 18-day moving average). When the fast moving average is above the slow moving average, the trend is assumed to be up. A buy signal is generated when the fast moving average crosses from below to above the slow moving average. A sell signal is generated when the fast moving average crosses from above to below the slow moving average.

There are numerous other moving average types and systems. An exponential moving average adds greater weight to the latest data in the series, thus responding to changes faster

Continued next page

than a simple moving average. It also does not jump as sharply when an old outlier falls off the chart.

The exponential moving average is calculated as follows:

$$EMA = C(K) + (EMA_{-1})(1 - K),$$

where

$K = 2/(n + 1)$

n = the number of days in the exponential moving average

C = today's closing price

EMA_{-1} = the EMA of yesterday
(or the MA of yesterday if starting at the beginning of a data series).

Hence, to *calculate* an exponential moving average over a five-day period, K equals $2/(5 + 1) = 2/6 = 0.333$. The closing prices of the first five days are added and divided by five in order to find the moving average of those first five days. Then, on day six, the closing price is multiplied by 0.333 and yesterday's moving average is added and multiplied by 0.667.

TRADING
WITH
THE ODDS

USING THE POWER OF
PROBABILITY TO
PROFIT IN THE
FUTURES MARKET

CHAPTER 1

Increasing the Probability of Success with Science and Statistics

The Kase methods specifically address issues of maintaining profitability while lowering risk and simplifying trading methodology, focusing on the concerns of those traders who are not in a position either professionally or economically to trade a diverse portfolio of commodities. This chapter reviews the basic philosophy and understanding that underlies the methods provided in this book.

REPLACE EMPIRICAL METHODS WITH MATHEMATICALLY DERIVED MODELS

Older empirical techniques have been replaced with mathematically sound techniques derived from the natural structure of the markets. Most of the popular technical indicators used today were developed prior to the introduction of even the most basic of personal computers (PCs).

MANIPULATE DATA TO IMPROVE PERFORMANCE

Some of the limitations of the current ways data is displayed and analyzed can be overcome by modifying and adjusting the data using the power available from computer technology.

CONDENSE INFORMATION

Traders can limit errors of judgment and free themselves to consider strategic issues by programming the computer to perform routine calculations, and the information gathered can be condensed by use of Pareto's Law. This law of the *trivial many* and the *critical few*, or the 80/20 law, was developed by Italian-Swiss engineer and economist Vilfredo Pareto (1848–1923), who believed that income dis-

1

tribution is constant, historically and geographically, regardless of external economic pressures and that a small percentage of the workforce produces most of the output. For example, 20 percent of traders generate 80 percent of revenues, and 20 percent of the population holds 80 percent of the land.

To apply Pareto's law to trading, traders should process the most useful indicator information, disregarding more trivial details. In terms of technical analysis, 20 percent of what can be programmed about an indicator or technique will capture 80 percent of the value of that technique. Therefore, to examine a single indicator, 80 percent of our effort is used to understand the last 20 percent of detail. Instead, five indicators may be programmed to capture 80 percent of the value of each. Using the same amount of effort, the scope with which the market can be viewed increases by 400 percent.

AUTOMATICALLY ADAPTIVE INDICATORS

Indicators can be designed that adapt automatically to changing market conditions, such as volatility, the variation in volatility, and cycle or trend lengths.

Studies have shown that optimization of simple indicators and systems, generally speaking, does not work. Optimization is the process of back-testing a system over historical data to determine the precise values for its parameters that, historically, produce the most profit. Optimization assumes that what worked in the past will work in the future. In reality, the market breathes and moves and expands and contracts in such a way that the cycles and volatility change. Thus, any system optimized for a certain set of market conditions over a small number of commodities or time-frames is not particularly effective. A system that works over a long time-frame must be either a blunt instrument system that requires diversification to limit risk or a highly accurate system that automatically adapts itself to market conditions and, through such adaptation, reduces risk. Many traders are not in a position to trade a "basket" of commodities. They are either employed to trade a small number of commodities or do not have the capital, as private traders, to diversify.

Therefore, to achieve a highly accurate, lower-risk trading style suitable for trading a small number of commodities, the accuracy of one's techniques must be improved. This is accomplished by improving the mathematical and logical bases for such techniques. In this context, we use diversity to minimize risk by trading multiple time-frames, using more complex and statistically accurate technical analyses without increasing the strain on the trader performing such analyses.

To do this, we must make full use of the power and computational speed of PCs available to us, not only to analyze market information, but also to condense it into a more utilitarian format for the trader. We must also increase accuracy by designing indicators that adjust automatically to market conditions and by fine-tuning traders' timing, i.e., when to enter a trade and, even more critically, when to exit.

SCIENCE, NOT MAGIC

There is general consensus among students of the markets that, for reasonable lengths of time, the markets exhibit behaviors that cannot be considered random or independent of a previous event in a given time period. Not too long ago, in the minds of many people, technical analysis was a field rated barely above numerology and perhaps a rung or two below alchemy. Today, those same critics are beginning to acknowledge that the study of the markets from a logical, rational, scientific perspective is a valid field of inquiry—and one also with high stakes. In October 1993, the *Economist* magazine published a survey on mathematics of the market. This rather lengthy survey noted that Wall Street was becoming populated with physical scientists and engineers, men and women who spend their professional careers quantifying events and elements in pursuit of patterns that help them understand the nature of the universe.

Some resist the idea that quantifying market behavior—or any behavior—is possible. This is hardly surprising; many people resisted the ideas of Sir Isaac Newton when he described laws pertaining to the physical universe some 200 years ago. Likewise, Copernicus and Galileo met great skepticism when they employed the principles we take for granted today. We know that novelty and validity are not always related, and so, some ideas that challenge existing beliefs can be difficult to accept.

Describing the physical universe using quantitative terms has become a part of everyday life, yet describing the behavioral universe quantitatively is still something that many find uncomfortable. They see behavior as a matter of spontaneity and free choice. Quantification, however, implies patterns and order. Spontaneity and free choice exist within a patterned and ordered framework that is defined by certain laws.

NEW IDEAS CHALLENGE OLD BELIEFS

Reality is the trader's friend. Seeking market truth requires an open mind and a confidence in one's own foundation, so that new ideas will strengthen that foundation.

This book strives to understand the insensate, behavioral universe and the physical, measurable universe on the same terms, with the same scientific and mathematical rigor, utilizing the same types of analytical tools. Today we have access to excellent calculating and programming tools to quantify and study behavior. The study of mass behavior and mathematics has continued to mesh since Robert Malthus published his landmark work, *An Essay on the Principle of Population*, in 1820. A Cambridge-trained mathematician and economist, Malthus drew many parallels between mass behavior and classical physics, often proving his claims to a mathematical certainty.

As applied to the market, human behavior is indicated by price activity and its derivatives, such as volatility and volume. These are mathematical abstractions of this behavior; the human reactions to combinations of events relating to specific markets and to the physical universe. Traders can use the most modern tools to examine the markets scientifically and analyze this derived data in order to paint an accurate picture of market movements.

This scientific approach is not beyond the reach of those with a basic foundation in math or logical thinking. There is hope for those of us who have had difficulty with polymer chemistry and partial differential equations. The market itself is not precise enough from the standpoint of the futures trader to require more than an understanding of the most basic concepts in elementary physics and introductory statistics. More important, is a commitment to logic and a good conceptual grasp of the structures and behavior of the market, i.e., *mathematical intuition*.

CORPORATE TRADING MUST BE ACCURATE

My background as a corporate trader greatly influenced my trading style, philosophy, and approach. This has had two major ramifications: a commitment to low-risk style and the use of trading techniques that can be simplified by the computer.

As a corporate trader, I traded a single market or a group of related markets and was burdened with a high degree of corporate scrutiny. Often, fund managers use a technique that might be characterized as a blunt instrument approach. They need not be very accurate because they are trading a basket of different commodities, minimizing risk by choosing commodities whose movements offset each other. They stop out the losers and ride winning trades. These diversification methods are, of course, by definition, not available to most corporate traders.

In a conservative corporate environment, managers of trading departments often maintain their supervisory positions because they have proven themselves in other corporate departments. They generally have little or no experience in actual trading, so the concept that a good trader may experience a string of small losses and still make money is difficult to grasp. They often fail to understand that sometimes the market is more difficult to trade, for example, during choppy sideways consolidations than, at other times, for example during prolonged trends. Thus, they instruct traders under their supervision with an impossible dual message: "Make money most of the time, during all market conditions, taking very little risk."

The indicators and trading methods discussed in this book have been formed by my experience in such conservative, risk-adverse corporate and institutional environments, in which traders must not only generate profit, but also limit losses.

When trading a single commodity, the risk cannot be spread over a basket of commodities, so losers cannot be stopped out while letting the winners run. The corporate environment cannot abide a high-risk trading style, even if that style generates high rewards. A style that may generate a series of many, albeit modest, consecutive losses is unacceptable. A highly accurate trading style is a must.

Richard Donchian, in the December 1974 issue of *Commodities* magazine (the precursor of *Futures* magazine), wrote on the subject of 5- and 20-day moving averages. I learned a great deal from this article and developed a number of rules for my own trading (referred to repeatedly in this book). Donchian tested a wide variety of commodities over just less than a 14-year history. No single commodity was profitable each year and of 28 commodities, 8 lost money over the entire 14-year span and 20 made money. The moving average system Donchian tested made money 9 out of the 14 years. Donchian strongly suggested that the way to overcome the fact that certain commodities lose money in such systems is to diversify, which, he said, lessens risk.

In the course of his study, which spanned 1961 to 1973, Donchian found soybeans to be the most profitable commodity to trade using his method. However, soybeans actually lost money during 7 of the 14 years. One losing stretch, for example, spanned 4 years in a row, from 1967 to 1970. No trader employed by a commodity house to trade soybeans would hold his job during this four-year period, under those circumstances. Similar studies, using other indicators, have shown results consistent with Donchian's. Clearly then, blunt instrument methodologies are not appropriate for single-commodity traders, whose specific task it is to make money in a single market or hedge a particular commodity.

The difference between trading a portfolio and trading a single commodity can be seen in the illustration of Trader A and Trader B. Both are correct 40 percent of the time and have a 2-to-1 win/loss ratio. Trader A has 50 coins and each coin toss has a 40 percent probability of coming up heads and a 60 percent probability of coming up tails. If a coin comes up heads, he wins two dollars; if a coin comes up tails, he loses one dollar. Trader B is given the same 50 coins and has the same win/loss costs. The difference is that

Trader A is allowed to toss all 50 coins at once while Trader B must toss each coin individually and consecutively. If either trader loses two dollars, he will lose his job.

The odds are vastly in favor of Trader A, because the most likely probability is that he will make two dollars on 40 percent of the coins and lose one dollar on 60 percent of the coins for a profit of $10. For Trader B, however, each sequential toss has a 60 percent chance of coming up tails and a 36 percent chance of having two losses in a row. A portfolio trader, as Trader A, can toss all the coins in the air at the same time, while a single-market trader, as Trader B, must rely on the outcome of one toss at a time. Obviously, both the techniques and methods of evaluation must be different for the two different traders.

WHILE NEVER EASY, TRADING CAN AT LEAST BE SIMPLE

Many corporate traders are transferred into trading with absolutely no prior experience. Most begin managing millions of dollars of commodity exposure without even a rudimentary knowledge of technical analysis. They view in-house trading positions as temporary assignments on the way up the corporate ladder and often rely on outside professional advisors for weekly strategies and analyses.

Some traders face information overload and feel they cannot deal with one more piece of data as they seek to trade a commodity, buy and sell the commodity to "balance the system," meet with customers, negotiate term contracts, and attend to a multitude of administrative responsibilities. Thus, any simplification and automation of the trading process is an enormous benefit to them.

It should be noted that I am not speaking of "black-box" systems (automated trading systems are generally considered *taboo* and distrusted in corporate environs), but rather an improvement and partial automation of the *tools* traders use to move towards their goals. The fastest sportscar won't get you where you want to go if you are wearing a blindfold. However, given equivalent drivers, the one with a well-planned route, some on-line directions, and a better car, will win. One need not know all the mechanics of engines and transmissions to operate a vehicle. One must only know how to drive!

CHAPTER 2

The True Nature
of the Market

The following chapters look at a new series of technical indicators that take advantage of both the computing capability available today and a statistical and scientific understanding of the market. First, some basic premises about the market need to be addressed.

WHAT IS IMPORTANT TO
UNDERSTAND ABOUT THE MARKET?

The Market Is Symmetrical Across Time-frames

First, the market is fractally symmetrical, meaning that, at different levels, the market looks the same. A set of Russian dolls provides a good illustration of this concept. A Russian doll set contains increasingly smaller dolls inside each doll. When the biggest doll is opened, a smaller, duplicate doll is found inside. When that smaller doll is opened, another still smaller doll is found inside. The third doll opens to a fourth, which opens to a fifth, until the last doll is too small. The market is similar.

Second, most of us think about the market in terms of time. If we review and evaluate the market on a monthly basis, for example, we see certain patterns, trends, and formations; and if we look at charts on a weekly, daily, hourly, or 15-minute basis, we see the same patterns. Although there are some differences between long-term charts and short-term charts (e.g., a tick chart that notes every single price change that has taken place in the market), they are more similar than dissimilar and exhibit the same patterns and behaviors. In many instances, if the x-axis is not labeled, one cannot tell the difference between a 15-minute chart and a daily chart.

The key to the symmetry and the point at which a break between the macro and micro market levels occur is the level of activity at each interval. If every interval or bar on a chart captures a microcosm or story of human behavior (fear, greed, and, hopefully, some rational activity), then, provided the time interval is long enough to contain an entire story, we can operate at the macro level of the market. A story may encompass months or moments, but it must have a recognizable beginning, middle and end. When the level of activity within a certain time-frame is incomplete, i.e., the time-frame or interval is not long enough to contain a complete story, we enter the micro level of the market. Nevertheless, in broad terms, the market looks the same at all levels.

Elliott's Wave Theory Is Essentially Correct

A corollary is R.N. Elliott's Wave Theory. In the 1930s, Elliott developed the theory that price activity is basically a representation of mass psychology; thus, plotted price activity of the markets drew a picture of how people behave. Elliott looked at the patterns that developed rather than the time-frames in which the patterns occurred and found that these patterns formed waves. He quantified these seemingly random waves of price activity and classified them into particular graphic patterns. Mass psychological behavior, he believed, is a structurally repetitive phenomenon that obeys natural laws of progression. Many people take issue with the validity and usefulness of the Elliott Wave Theory and berate Elliott Wave practitioners for changing wave counts and constantly updating their market views. Notwithstanding such particulars, Elliott's theories about the market in general, and his view that there is a natural law that governs the market, are correct in broad terms.

Forecasting versus Trading

Forecasting and trading are two different activities. Forecasting can be defined as projecting price activity into the future using past and present price activity. Trading, on the other hand, is the actual carrying out of a transaction of buying and selling a stock, bond, or futures contract.

The value of forecasting is similar to the value of drawing a map or getting directions before driving from point A to point B. The Elliott Wave Theory serves the trader as a broad-based map of the markets that provides the trader with a better chance of arriving at his or her destination without getting lost *en route*. However, maps don't take into consideration traffic jams, road blocks, detours, etc. A driver must use common sense to navigate between what is beyond the windshield in the real, physical world and where the map directs him to go. Drivers adapt their routes if there is a conflict between map directions and what is actually visible on the road ahead. Similarly, a trader must constantly observe the actual price activity, while referring to the forecast for general directions.

I have found that Elliott Wave patterns are generally applicable all the way down to the tick level and that it is always better for a trader to utilize such a road map as this as opposed to solely relying upon individual road signs along the way.

The Market Is Mostly Predictable

I also believe that active markets, which are widely traded, are generally predictable, though never entirely. The most predictable markets are those not dominated by any one particular entity or small group of entities and those not regulated. The laws of mass psychology apply to these markets. Markets, such as corn and heating oil, which depend in large measure upon natural environmental factors, are also highly predictable. If we lived under a different economic regime, people and animals would still eat corn, which would grow best at certain times of the year, and they would use fuel, which would still be required to heat homes during cold weather. In opposition, we have financial instruments, such as shares of stock in a small company whose product may be "synthetic" (the advisory services of a large accounting firm, for example). If our economic system were to change or if the principal parties of such a firm were to vanish, the value or existence of the entity would be voided. Such markets and instruments are less predictable because they can be significantly influenced by fairly insignificant events.

In forecasting, our objective is to know what is knowable and humbly accept that we cannot know everything. Despite the fact that the probabilities favor an understanding of the market most of the time, we can never know all there is to know. Human beings are fallible and can only understand the market to the extent that it understands itself. We cannot foresee the unforeseen, such as hurricanes, assassinations, law suits, deaths, and all other events that we can lump under the general heading of *force majeure* or acts of God.

Since markets are driven by human behavior, we can think about the predictability of a market in the same way we might think about the predictability of any type of human behavior. We can make generalizations if we know a person or a particular group of people well, and, as a result, we can often predict behavior in a general sense. We might not be able to predict the exact words a person will say, but rather, the general concept of what he or she will express. In the same way, we can make general predictions or forecasts about the market, while recognizing that, since people in our society have free will and are able to act in ways that are unpredictable, the market itself will behave in an unpredictable fashion from time to time.

Market Extremes Are Unstable and Unpredictable

All market properties are skewed to the right, since many market properties are bound on the downside by zero. Price cannot be negative. Absolute percentage rate of change in the market cannot be negative. On the other hand, price spikes (or outliers), when compared to average or normal prices, can be extreme, as can spikes or outliers in volatility.

The markets are skewed to the right (positively), meaning that the median, or exact center of the data set, is to the left of the mean or average of those data points. Outlier(s) are to the right (see Chapter Two Appendix, "Statistics Overview").

Rate of change in price can be high and spike to the upside but can never be less than zero. Volatility can be greater than 100 percent but can never be less than zero. We can know, with certainty, what the left hand boundaries of our graphs are, but the right hand side may be theoretically infinite. Our task, as forecasters, is to determine reasonable limits within which the vast portion of the right hand side of the graphs will be contained. This uncertainty on the right side of the curve shows us our limitations as human beings and constitutes the boundary of what can be known and what can never be known about the markets.

The Logarithmic Spiral Describes Market Behavior

Our next corollary is that logarithmic spirals, Fibonacci series and Fibonacci ratios, are descriptive of market behavior. In the 13th century, Leonardo Fibonacci rediscovered a number sequence that had been used by the ancient Greeks and Egyptians in the construction of such edifices as the Parthenon and the Great Pyramids. The sequence of numbers begins with 1, adds a second 1, then sums the first two numbers to arrive at the third number, i.e., 2. From that point, each two sequential numbers are added together to arrive at the next number in the series: 1, 1, 2, 3, 5, 8, 13, 21, 34, and so on.

This sequence has some interesting characteristics, the most important being that, after the first four numbers, the ratio of each number in the series to the next highest number approaches 0.618. The Greeks called this number the Golden Ratio, which is the basis of the logarithmic spiral we see in such natural constructions as snail shells.

Why the markets conform to these numbers is as difficult to explain as it would be to ask a snail why its shell forms spirals. However, the absence of a fully explicable "why" does not alter the observable reality. This is another of those situations in which we must accept the limitations of what it is possible to know. Our goal is simply to make accurate and objective observations.

There Is No Magic Formula or Easy Answer

Our final assumption is that there is no perfect system. The best we can hope for is to understand the understandable, to predict the predictable, and to harness those aspects of the market that behave in conjunction with or in accordance with generalized, recognized patterns and the expectations derived from those patterns. What a logical, statistical, scientific approach to technical analysis and trading can do is cut as close as possible to the edge of predictability, to the precipice between that portion of the market that is predictable and understandable and the chaos beyond.

Statistics Overview

Statistics, in general, is the branch of mathematics that gives descriptions to, and draws conclusions from, numerical observations. It involves the descriptive measure of a sample. Statistics can be expressed either numerically or pictorially. In general, statistics are used to look at two types of numerical measures, the measure of central tendency, the middle of a certain set of observations or values, and the measure of variability, how far from that center point the observations stray. *Mean* and *median* are two measures of central tendency.

MEAN

The most commonly used statistical term is mean, which is the average for a set of data and is an indicator for central tendency. The formula for mean is:

$$Mean = \frac{1}{n} \sum x_i$$

where x is all the variables to be considered and n is the number of variables included in the sample. Mean is calculated by adding the values of all the variables in a sample and dividing by the number (or quantity) of the variables themselves.

Let's assume that two students are taking a statistics class. Student A and Student B have the following seven test scores:

Student A: 82%, 70%, 72%, 85%, 94%, 90%, 88%
Student B: 91%, 74%, 80%, 87%, 85%, 83%, 81%

For Students A and B, their means are:

A: Mean $= [\frac{1}{7} \times (82\% + 70\% + 72\% + 85\% + 94\% + 90\% + 88\%)] = 83\%$

B: Mean $= [\frac{1}{7} \times (91\% + 74\% + 80\% + 87\% + 85\% + 83\% + 81\%)] = 83\%$

In this example, both Student A and Student B have a mean score of 83 percent.

OUTLIERS

The main problem with calculating the mean is the influence of outliers. An outlier is an abnormal or unusual data point. Using the previous example, let's assume one of our students had a test score of 30 percent. The 30 percent is considered an outlier because it is far out of the range of all the other test scores, which for both students was above 70 percent.

MEDIAN

To get a better measure of central tendency, the median should be calculated in addition to the mean. The median is the data point located in the middle of a data set after the data has been arranged in an ascending order from the smallest to the largest. Test scores are:

Student A: 70%, 72%, 82%, 85%, 88%, 90%, 94%

Student B: 74%, 80%, 81%, 83%, 85%, 87%, 91%

Student A has a median of 85 percent and Student B has a median of 83 percent.

For this example, the median was easily located because there is an odd quantity of test scores. However, if there had been eight test scores instead of seven, the numbers would be arranged in ascending order and the average interpolated between the two middle scores.

Example: Test scores are: 65%, 68%, 75%, 79%, 85%, 88%, 95%, 98%. The median is 82%, calculated as follows:

$$\frac{(79\% + 85\%)}{2} = 82\%$$

MEASURE OF VARIABILITY

The mean and median are two measures of central tendency. Because central tendency is only a partial representation of data analysis, variability (also known as spread) should also be determined. Variability can be measured by *range, variance*, and *standard deviation*.

RANGE

The easiest way to measure variability is range, which is the difference between the smallest and largest number of a data set:

A: 94% − 70% = 24

B: 91% − 74% = 17

Although range is the easiest measure of variability, it is limited because two different data sets could have the same range, though their variabilities could differ drastically. The extremes of the two sets would simply have to be equidistant. Range does not take into consideration the possibility of outliers. Because of this limitation, variance and standard deviation are usually measured in addition to range.

VARIANCE

Variance and standard deviation are used to measure variability around the mean. Deviation here means the distance of the measurements from the mean of the sample.

Variance is the sum of the squared deviation scores (*x minus the Mean for all values of x*) divided by $n - 1$ (*where n is the number of values in the sample*). The formula for variance is:

$$s^2 = \frac{1}{n-1} \sum (x - Mean)^2$$

Since the mean is the exact middle of the distribution, the weight of the combined samples both above and below the mean are identical. To arrive at a meaningful result, the terms of the equation must be squared. The sum of the difference between the number and the mean will always be zero, as the following examples indicate.

A: [(70% − 83%) + (72% − 83%) + (82% − 83%) + (85% − 83%) +
     (88% − 83%) + (90% − 83%) + (94% − 83%)] =
     [(−13%) + (−11%) + (−1%) + (2%) + (5%) + (7%) + (11%)] = 0%

B: [(74% − 83%) + (80% − 83%) + (81% − 83%) + (83% − 83%) +
     (85% − 83%) + (87% − 83%) + (91% − 83%)] =
     [(−9%) + (−3%) + (−2%) + (0%) + (2%) + (4%) + (8%)] = 0%

The variances* for Student A and Student B are:

Student A

$$\frac{1}{7-1}[(.70 - .83)^2 + (.72 - .83)^2 + (.82 - .83)^2 + (.85 - .83)^2 +$$

$$(.88 - .83)^2 + (.90 - .83)^2 + (.94 - .83)^2] = \frac{1}{6}(.049) = 8.166 \times 10^{-3}$$

Student B

$$\frac{1}{7-1}[(.74 - .83)^2 + (.80 - .83)^2 + (.81 - .83)^2 + (.83 - .83)^2 +$$

$$(.85 - .83)^2 + (.87 - .83)^2 + (.91 - .83)^2] = \frac{1}{6}(.0187) = 3.117 \times 10^{-3}$$

---

*The test scores are converted from percent to decimal form because percentages do not represent actual units.

STANDARD DEVIATION

Standard deviation is the square root of variance. Standard deviation is important because variance uses squared units (i.e., inches^2, dollars^2, etc.), while standard deviation uses actual units. Using the variance from our Student A and Student B example:

$$A: \; s.\,dev \; = \; \sqrt{8.1667 \times 10^{-3}}$$

$$A: \; s.\,dev \; = \; .09036$$

$$B: \; s.\,dev \; = \; \sqrt{3.117 \times 10^{-3}}$$

$$B: \; s.\,dev \; = \; .0558$$

The smaller the standard deviation, the more tightly the measurements in a sample tend to cluster around the "middle." The variance and standard deviation for both students prove that Student B is more consistent in his test scoring. Statistical descriptions are often expressed as a number of standard deviations from the mean. So, for Student A, one standard deviation around the mean (of 83 percent) would signify the range from 83 percent minus 9.036 percent or 74 percent to 83 percent plus 9.036 percent or 92 percent.

STEM AND LEAF

The statistical analyses of Student A and Student B can be taken one step further by using various graphs, the easiest being the stem and leaf, also known as a stemplot. The stem and leaf method takes the first digit of each score for the stem and uses the remaining digits as leaves. If two sequential scores have the same first digit, leaves are added to the first stem. When the first digit of the next sequential score is different from the predecessor, it is a new stem. So, for Student A, the first stem would be 7 with 0 and 2 as its leaves, forming 7 | 0 2. For Student B, the first stem would be 7, and the leaf would be 4 to form 7 | 4. The stems and leaves for Student A and Student B would appear:

Student A		Student B	
7	0 2	7	4
8	2 5 8	8	0 1 3 5 7
9	0 4	9	1

The stem and leaf graph for both students indicates that each should have means in the 80s because the eight stem has more leaves (test scores) than the seven stem or nine stem, respectively.

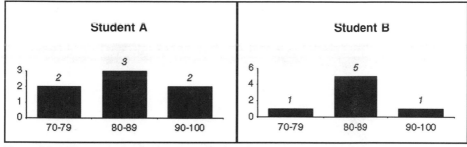

Figure 2A–1 Histograms for Student A and Student B

HISTOGRAM

The stem and leaf method can be taken one step further by creating a histogram, a bar graph that indicates the frequency for a given range (i.e., how many test scores fell within the range that qualifies for an "A"). Our student example generates the histograms in Figure 2A–1.

NORMAL DISTRIBUTION

The histograms for both students indicate that there is a normal distribution among the students' test scores. A normal distribution is referred to as a bell curve because if a line is drawn around the outside edges of the bars, it will, theoretically, look like a bell, weighted evenly on each side (see Figure 2A–2). The downward arrow indicates the location of the mean and the median.

Because the bell curve (normal distribution) has equal amounts of data on each side of the mean, one standard deviation is defined as 33.3 percent of the data. Hence, the following characteristics are true for any type of bell curve:

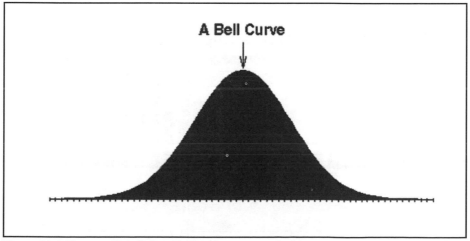

Figure 2A–2 The normal or "Bell" curve

a) Approximately 67 percent of all the data will be within ± one standard deviation of the mean.

b) Approximately 95 percent of all data will be within ± two standard deviations of the mean.

c) Approximately 99.7 percent of all data will be within ± three standard deviations of the mean.

CUMULATIVE DISTRIBUTION

Although the normal distribution displays data well in many cases, a cumulative distribution may be required. A cumulative distribution graph displays the data in a cumulative process, where the x-axis represents the sample and the y-axis represents the percentage of the total data. The highest y-axis value is 1.0 (or 100 percent of the total data). The cumulative distribution from zero to the mean is 50 percent on a normal distribution curve. The cumulative distribution from zero to a positive one standard deviation is 50 percent plus 33.3 percent or 83.3 percent. The cumulative distribution from zero to a negative one standard deviation is 50 percent minus 33.3 percent or 16.7 percent. While a normal distribution creates a bell curve, the cumulative distribution usually creates a step function, as in Figure 2A–3. The following graph illustrates that, as the number of hours increases for a day, the percentage that the hours represent per day also increases. One hour out of a day is equivalent to .04 (four percent) of a day while 23 hours is equivalent to .96 (96 percent) of a day.

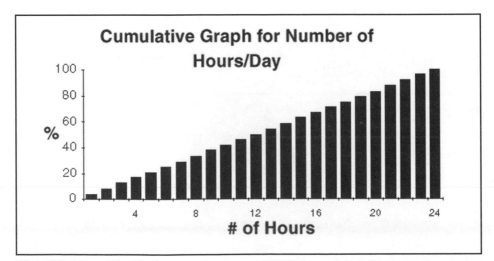

Figure 2A–3 Cumulative Histogram

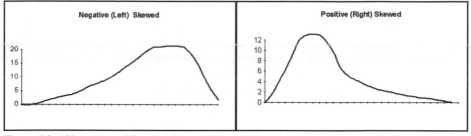

Figure 2A–4 Negative and Positive Skewed Distributions

SKEW

Distributions in which a data sample does not produce a normal bell curve are referred to as skewed. Skew occurs when a data sample has outliers. A data set can be skewed to the right (positively) or the left (negatively). If data is positively skewed, the median will be to the left of the mean on the graph and outliers will be to the right.

   If the data is skewed to the left (negative), the median will be to the right of the mean and outliers will be to the left.

DEPENDENT VARIABLE OR EVENT

The dependent variable is a variable or an event that *depends* on another variable or event. It is caused by or influenced by another variable. The outcome of one dependent event has an effect on the probability of the outcome of the other.

INDEPENDENT VARIABLES OR EVENTS

An independent variable causes or effects other variables. Other variables depend on it. Independent events are stand alone events that have no effect on and are not influenced by other events.

CHAPTER 3

Developing a Strategy with
Accurate Forecasting

Forecasting techniques allow traders to bias their trading and timing in a particular direction and alerts them to possible market turns or decision points in the market. Analyzing the direction of the market and incorporating forecasting techniques into the trading game plan are not easy tasks. As is true in any endeavor that has high potential reward, forecasting and strategy design tend to attract the most aggressive and most determined competitors. The solace is that no matter how smart or intuitive the competition may be, better tools and hard work ultimately provide the edge.

The information presented here is oriented toward the serious professional trader and the committed private trader, who are willing to take the time and make the effort necessary to prepare a well-designed trading strategy. There are no simplistic or easy answers. There is no magic program that will propel traders into the realm of an eight-figure income overnight. While trading itself (market timing) should be easy and mechanical, a great deal of hard work and preparation is required before getting to the easy part. Traders who are willing to analyze the market, incorporate forecasting techniques, and design a well thought out money management and trading plan will have an edge over traders who are looking for a fast, easy way out. This hard work and market analysis should be done when the market is closed, eliminating the pressure of making critical decisions in the heat of battle.

CAN PEOPLE REALLY
FORECAST THE MARKET ACCURATELY?

The markets are basically a numerical and graphical representation of mass psychology. Traders see patterns within the behavior of the markets and, with practice, learn to recognize familiar patterns and anticipate reactions to them. It takes a lot of practice, and it is difficult to program such patterns into a computer because the variables can often be rather vague. We have all seen examples of this reality in other walks of life. An obstetrician can count fingers and toes on an ultrasound of a fetus, while most of us just see a blob. Geologists pick high potential drill sites by evaluating patterns formed by erratic, squiggly seismic lines. Likewise, accurately recognizing and interpreting geometrical reversal (or, more descriptively, non-continuation) patterns in the market structure is as practiced. However, it is well worth the effort and can provide a dedicated trader with an edge over the competition.

Proof that people can and do forecast the market lies in my own experience. I forecast the energy market every week. Since October, 1993 my weekly results in calling market direction and turns have been documented at just less than 90 percent accuracy. I have also been about 70 percent accurate in calling exact price (to within points) of the specific levels at which the market would turn. To use a well-worn phrase, "the proof of the pudding is in the eating." What better proof that a market is predictable than a proven track record of predictions?

Some markets are easier to forecast than others. It behooves us, as traders interested in profit rather than self-aggrandizement, to look for markets that exhibit certain characteristics. I forecast the energy market, partly, because I have some expertise in the field. I suggest that, in order to develop a high degree of accuracy in a particular market, traders should focus on a small group of markets, become familiar with them, and look for characteristics that are manageable within them. Specifically, they should:

1. Look for a market that is more or less mean-reverting in the medium-term, in the sense that it tends to revert to an average or a norm. As a result, prices are held in a definable and understandable, though sometimes rather wide, trading range.

2. Choose a market that, while being subject to some degree of influence by random natural events, such as the vagaries of weather, is rarely affected by political or purely random events.

3. Look for an active and liquid market that is dominated by traders who do not use technical analysis to any great degree.

THE SIX KASE BEHAVIORAL LAWS OF FORECASTING

Before beginning to trade, a trader must have a clear idea of the precise goals, from a business standpoint, that he is attempting to achieve. A psychological viewpoint that addresses those objectives in a practical and attainable fashion must be established. There are six behavioral laws that all traders who want to be successful should learn and practice.

Law Number One: *Remember that the objective is profit, not ego-stroking.*

It is more important to be long when the market is rising and short when the market is falling than to forecast the exact high or low of a move. Too many forecasters are sidetracked by thinking that the objective of their work is to be correct on calling the market. They forget that correct calls on market direction must be included within a comprehensive trading strategy in order to be effective.

Any technically based strategy for trading markets generates a number of signals or patterns that indicate either that the status quo will perpetuate (the trend will continue) or that something is about to change (a correction or reversal is about to take place). The difficulty in trading the "right edge" of the chart is knowing which signals to act on immediately and which indicate simply to "pay attention here" and wait for a confirmation of some sort.

Trading strategies should make use of forecasts. When a signal occurs in the direction of the trend or follows a clearly defined turn, such as a spike top or V-bottom confirmed by a combination of indicators (see Chapter 5, "Market Turns"), and does so when it is near a node or failure point, it can be acted on immediately; in other words, a trader may take the trade. The signal itself is a confirmation of something that is already occurring in the market. If signals occur in the *opposite* direction of a major trend, which most likely means that the market may be moving into a corrective phase, a trader should wait for a second signal to confirm the first. Often corrections are short-lived, so a second signal, usually following a pull-back, is needed to confirm that the correction is of a quality and duration suitable for trading.

In summary, first signals in the direction of the trend or after clear turns should be taken; otherwise traders should wait for second signals. The market will tell us everything we need to know about it.

Law Number Two: *The objective is profitable trading, not proving a thesis or world view.*

I consider the Elliott Wave Theory to be a basic structure that assists in making accurate forecasts and conducting profitable trading strategies. Just as gravity pulls objects toward the center of the earth and we can act with confidence that a falling object will travel downward (though we may not know exactly where it will land), traders should not debate the minute details of a thesis but keep their focus on the goals of controlling risk and generating profit.

While I acknowledge that Elliott was fundamentally correct (see Chapter 2), I also recognize that his theory is not carved in stone. The minutiae of his theory have sparked heated debates. His contributions are subject to revision and improvement.

Law Number Three: *When wrong, move on.*

Those who seek perfection can never achieve true success. Perfection is always elusive. The only way never to be wrong and never suffer a loss is to avoid forecasting and trading altogether. It is impossible for a trader to be any good unless he is willing to be wrong. A trader can succeed only if he is willing to risk failure within the constraints of his defined trading plan or system.

Oppenheimer said that one of the proofs of Einstein's greatness was that it took others 10 years to correct his errors. We all make mistakes; even Einstein did. The keys are learning to accept that fallibility and remembering that our aim is profitable trading and not saving face or impressing other people. This attitude will help traders perform better as forecasters and traders.

All that anyone can know about the market is what it knows about itself. We can look at facts and make our own interpretations of those facts. Such things as wave counts depend on what is experienced, not what is divined. Where a particular wave lies in the sequence often depends on future unknowns, such as political or natural upheavals. It is important to maintain a fluid interpretation of Elliott's Wave Theory, rather than committing to a rigid one. The market itself is fluid and inexact. It is best to keep an open mind.

Law Number Four: *Have confidence in your own intuition. Do not rely on the advice or opinion of others, no matter how well respected they might be.*

Eighty percent of the money in the market is made by 20 percent of the people. If most people trading the markets consistently are incorrect and lose money, why bother asking for their opinions? This is absolutely self-defeating. John Kenneth Galbraith said it best when he observed that, when it comes to economic views, the majority is always wrong.

If you intend to be a good trader and an accurate forecaster, do not take a survey of market opinion. (If you do find a colleague who is consistently correct, either learn his system so that you can use his tools with your own intuition and experience or delegate part of your trading strategy development to him.) Remember that most people arrive at conclusions based on emotional bias, called "talking one's position," rather than by properly using a technical or fundamental approach.

Suggestion can be a powerful force, and the disposition to be influenced by the power of suggestion can be both a strength and a weakness. Some traders suggest successful methodologies to themselves. (For example, an impressionable person with a stress headache may be able to suggest to himself that his headache is psychosomatic and make the headache go away.) However, impressionability can also work to the traders' detriment: traders can be adversely influenced by suggestions from others (especially a boss). It is crucial that traders make up their own minds, based on their own observations and judgments.

Remember, the market will tell us all we need to know.

Law Number Five: *Do **not** read newspaper articles or watch newscasts that discuss the markets in which you have an interest.*

My favorite saying about trading commodities based on fundamental analysis is "to be a true fundamentalist, one needs the mind of God" in that God alone is omniscient and can take absolutely every detail into account. Many people are amazed that forecasters are able to call the market accurately without using fundamental analyses. However, most people who consider themselves fundamentalists are not true fundamentalists. Rather, they *speculate* on forecasts of fundamentals, such as what inventories will be, how many hurricanes will be experienced in a given season, and whether interest rates will be raised, as opposed to trading on "real" fundamental information. Also, many so-called fundamentalists have inaccurate, late, and incomplete information. Even those who have timely, relatively complete and accurate information are not always correct in their interpretations. They often miss the *market's* interpretation of actions such information will cause.

Technical analysis works on the assumption that all fundamental information is already reflected in the market's price. In a world in which information transfer is virtually instantaneous, anything that affects the markets (weather, shortages, supply/demand considerations, etc.) is almost instantaneously reflected in price, volume, velocity, acceleration, and volatility. Technical information is firsthand and immediate and takes into consideration all those myriad details it would take an omniscient being to monitor. Therefore, the technician has a much purer, unbiased, and complete view of what is actually happening in the real world market because the technician's information is based on the reactions of participants who have bought or sold, have their money on the line, and thus have a vested interest.

Law Number Six: *Plan your strategy when the market is closed—when you are rested and thinking clearly.*

Logical thinking and planning is best done when traders are not under pressure to trade. A professional football team, for example, must not only train but also diligently strategize together before each game. The team and its coaches try to anticipate every possible situation and prepare strategies that will turn those situations to their advantage. In the excitement of an actual game, they do not need to spend time devising strategies. They simply have to recognize a pattern and exercise the discipline to put a predetermined strategy into play. Traders must plan their strategies with the same diligence, after the market closes, when they have time to think, and not in the midst of actually trading, when emotions such as anger, fear, and greed can easily cloud judgment. They must plan what they will do under a variety of different circumstances, commit these plans and strategies to writing (even if only in note form), and have the discipline not to second guess themselves, but follow the plan. In other words, traders must *plan, not panic.*

MARKET GEOMETRY

Charles Dow compared the market to an ocean, with its waves and tidal ebbs and flows. I see the market more as a river, which moves and bends and splits into forks and tributaries. Smaller rivers also move and bend and split apart into streams and brooks, each of which behaves just as its larger parent. Rivers do not flow through perfectly straight channels. They are irregular, constantly changing to adapt to their environments. Within the irregularities of the river are other irregularities, but within all is a certain familiarity. Flowing water looks like flowing water, whether it is flowing around a mountain, a rock or a pebble. This is the essence of fractal geometry.

In the physical world, almost everything is fractal in nature, i.e., many things exhibit patterns that are evident at every level of observation. Depending on the technology applied, this fractal nature can be seen from many different points of view, each one providing a better understanding of the nature of reality. Careful examination of a snowflake with a magnifying glass reveals that all its delicate complexity is built around a simple triangle. A closer examination will show that triangle to be in the molecular structure of water itself.

The more sophisticated the tools with which we look at the markets, the more levels of understanding we can achieve. The river can be examined from an airplane flying at 50,000 feet that occasionally drops to tree level as well as by a student standing on its banks. Each will see the same patterns; but Elliott's wave patterns are identifiable in *both* macro and micro examinations of the markets.

A study of fractal analysis and chaos theory takes this analogy one step further. The river can be thought of in terms of following the path of a strange attractor that is in *equilibrium.* Equilibrium is an overall pattern, an idealized or optimum state, to which an otherwise chaotic environment is drawn.

Equilibrium is constantly changing and is generally only visible in macrocosm. The concept of strange attractors is that all chaotic systems tend toward some amorphous, idealized state. Rivers always head downward, flowing around mountains, through valleys, sometimes headed east, sometimes west, but always, eventually, to the sea. A river's tributary can be so small that a pebble would divert its path and cause yet another microcosm or meandering stream to form. However, if one flies far enough overhead to see the big picture, he will realize that the river follows a singular pattern and the streams never stray far from the overriding path.

There is no question that the markets are chaotic as well, but there is an overriding order that encompasses and incorporates all the spontaneity of the individual players within the mass crowd psychology. While indicators show the "physics" of the market, describing how events are predicated by other events and giving barometers with which to measure the market forces and concepts, such as Elliott Waves, addresses the overall shape, i.e., the order or the "geometry" to which the market tends.

FORECASTING METHODS

Following is the heart of techniques I use to forecast the market, the methods that work best.

The primary forecasting method that I use employs Elliott Waves along with a methodology called Fibonacci expansions and retracements and also incorporates analyses of several different types of gaps.

I have found that pattern techniques, such as head and shoulders, coils, and symmetrical triangles, are also useful. (Because their occurrence is rare, they are covered only briefly in Chapter 3 Appendix, "Using Chart Formations in Forecasting.")

Forecasting is both easy and difficult. The easy part is evaluating wave counts. This is easy in the sense that you either see it or you don't. Every artist sees patterns and shapes that others do not. An architect, for example, sees a home in a blueprint full of strange lines, radiologists see trauma in blotches on x-rays, and Michaelangelo saw David in a block of white marble. The ability to recognize visual patterns, which generally develops in childhood, is not so much learned as discovered, and, in truth, not everyone has it. The ability can be field specific. It is a talent and a gift. On the other hand, the ability can be developed with practice so that recognizing the patterns becomes trivial.

The basic idea in recognizing patterns for forecasting is to evaluate wave counts and try to determine the best estimate of where the market is in the count. It is especially important to know whether the market is in a trending or corrective move. The difficult and tedious part of forecasting is crunching a lot of numbers. In my own experience, I have found that there is a direct relationship between the degree of thoroughness in my evaluation of the calculations and the accuracy of my forecast.

Ultimately, we are looking for confluence numbers. When a situation is analyzed from many different perspectives and the numerical answers are consistently extremely close in value, these numbers confirm each other. For example, a market in a corrective phase that extends to a certain price, and whose price matches the price to which the correction phase of the previous move extended, is considered to be a confluence area.

When many paths or analysis methods lead to the same price, the confluence is high. The more paths, the higher the degree of confluence and the higher the probability that a particular price will at least be tested by the market.

Patterns and Rules

Next to be considered are the wave pattern rules of importance and the mathematics used to perform forecasts. Sometimes these rules are broken or modified to make them work better for us than the original Elliott Wave rules. All rules, of course, have exceptions, and market rules are no different. Therefore, the description of each rule, below, will also include situations under which rules either do not apply or should be modified.

The market trends in five waves and corrects in three.

Trending waves are formed by three impulse waves that move in the direction of the trend and two corrective waves against the trend (trending waves are generally labeled 1, 2, 3, 4, and 5). Clear corrections move in three waves, two in the direction of the correction and one against the correction (correcting waves are generally labeled *a*, *b*, and *c*).

This rule was developed for stock market indices and does not always hold true for commodities, which can be cyclical. In commodities, there may be five waves up and five waves down, forming a major cycle. Both commodities and futures have expiration dates, so there can be differing wave counts on the continuation charts versus the particular contract month charts. Traders may well find themselves in situations in which the chart of a particular contract month exhibits five waves that are, in reality, part of a 13-wave pattern once it is viewed on the continuation chart.

In commodities, traders use both continuation charts and individual contract month charts. Continuation charts are raw price charts and are never normalized when used for forecasting purposes. Close to expiration, it is important to look at the second or third next nearby contract. Upon expiration, aberrant behavior occurs more often than not, as people close out positions and contract volume drops off. If rules are broken upon expiration, the forecaster should be guided by the behavior of the second and third nearby deliverable contracts and discount the behavior of the first.

Wave 3 is never the smallest wave.

Wave 3 is most often the largest wave except when Wave 5 extends, i.e., takes on an elongated form that, under close examination, also exhibits at least five waves. Two of the waves are generally the same size (corollary: when any one of the three impulse waves extends, the other two impulse waves will be about the same size).

If Wave 2 is complex, i.e., erratic and choppy, Wave 4 will likely be simple, or vice versa. This is called the rule of alternation (a complex wave is almost always a corrective move).

This rule is both reliable and useful. In the energy markets, Wave 2 is almost always simple and Wave 4 is almost always complex. Continuation patterns, such as pennants, flags, ascending wedges, and the like, are all complex corrections. Technically, there are two types of patterns: reversal and continuation. The term reversal is a misnomer. While it implies a reversal in a trend, this is not necessarily so. It more accurately signals that a trend is to be interrupted for a time, either reversing or correcting in the opposite direction. A continuation pattern is a complex shallow correction, usually with a mild slope in opposition to the trend that it interrupts temporarily until the trend resumes or continues (see Chapter 3 Appendix, "Using Chart Formations in Forecasting," for a description of geometric chart patterns and their use in forecasting).

Complex corrections are simply too much trouble to trade. While it is possible to classify these corrections and fit them into wave counts, but I do not recommend focusing on this issue. This is one of those situations in which the best trade is no trade. Once a complex correction is recognized, the trader should stand aside.

The bottom of Wave 4 cannot fall below the bottom of Wave 2 in rising markets and vice versa on falling markets in which the top of Wave 4 cannot penetrate the top of Wave 2.

This rule is a slight modification of Elliott's original rule, which states that the bottom of Wave 4 should not penetrate Wave 1 (or the top of Wave 2) in up markets and vice versa in down markets. I have found that, when looking at commodities, Wave 4 often breaks through Wave 1. Even with this modified rule, I allow a couple of points of leeway in either direction. I also do not rely too heavily on this particular rule.

The market is fractally symmetrical, and, thus, each wave in the wave count also breaks down into five waves if trending and three waves if correcting.

That's it. Really. For all the books written about the Elliott Wave Theory, these simple rules, in conjunction with my own work, are really all you need to know to use this theory. It can help you forecast the market and increase your profitability.

The Math

There are three classes of mathematical formulae I use to forecast price: extensions, retracements, and the "rule of three." The extensions themselves break down into two subcategories: extensions that can be calculated based on impulse moves or on clean legs of corrective moves and extensions that can be calculated from corrections that have ended.

Figure 3–1 illustrates how all market moves that are relatively clean can be broken down into two pieces: an impulse piece and a corrective piece. The impulse piece moves from point X to point Y and the corrective piece travels downward to point Z, forming a three point group, $X\,Y\,Z$. The $X\,Y\,Z$ set will appear upside down in a bear market.

Points X, Y and Z here do not represent the waves themselves but rather the specific points that mark the beginnings and ends of those waves. This is not part of the traditional nomenclature but a construct that I use to identify specific numbers, points, or prices on the charts. Points X, Y, and Z indicate the extremes of any two waves beginning with an impulse wave. These waves can be either trending (Waves 1, 3, and 5) or correcting (Wave a and c).

For the first set of extensions, the difference in price between Y and X is multiplied by three different Fibonnacci ratios. These three differences in price are then projected in the direction of the trend from point Z, which will then be the beginning of the next impulse move. This provides three layers of projections: S (shorter than pre-

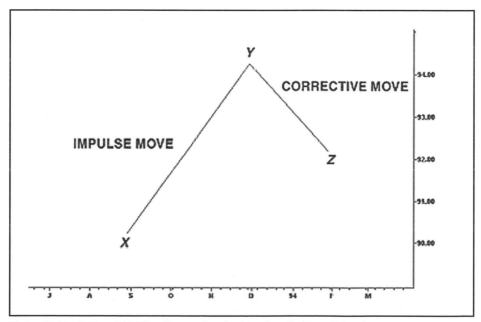

Figure 3–1 Definition of *XYZ* in a Forecasting System: Impulse Move Extensions

vious impulse move), E (equal to previous impulse move), and L (longer than previous impulse move).

For purposes of this forecasting technique, an impulse move is defined as either Waves 1, 3, and 5 of a trending formation or a simple Wave a or c of a corrective formation.

Smaller Than Rule: $S_{price} = Z_{price} + 0.618 (Y_{price} - X_{price})$

Equal To Rule: $E_{price} = Z_{price} + 1 (Y_{pric} - X_{price})$

Larger Than Rule: $L_{price} = Z_{price} + 1.618 (Y_{price} - X_{price})$

Corrective Move Retracements

The corrective move is the move from point Y to point Z. Thus, rather than looking at the price difference between the beginning of Wave 1 and the beginning of Wave 2 ($Y_{price} - X_{price}$), which is the length of Wave 1, forecasters should look at the price difference between the beginning of Wave 2 and the beginning of Wave 3 ($Y_{price} - Z_{price}$), which is the length of Wave 2.

The first extension is labeled "IT," which stands for " **I**f it's correcting the **T**hird wave." Most of the time, the third wave correction, Wave 4, will extend the next wave by 1.618 of the magnitude of the correction.

The second extension is labeled "IF," which stands for "**I**f it's correcting the **F**irst wave." Most often, the first wave correction in either a trending or corrective move (Wave 2, correcting Wave 1 in a

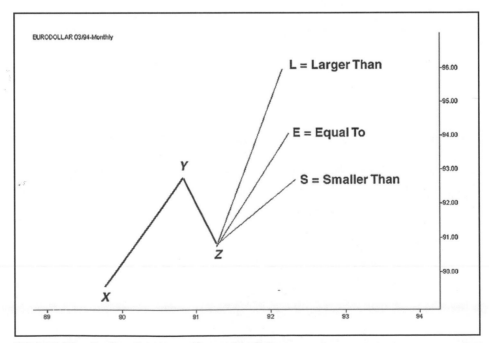

Figure 3–2 Smaller than, Equal to, and Larger than Rules

trending move or Wave b, correcting Wave a, in a corrective move) will extend by 1.618 squared.

The third extension is labeled "IX," which stands for "**I**f the market is correcting the first wave and it's e**X**tended beyond the IF magnitude." In this case, the extension is equivalent to the first wave correction times a factor of 1.618 cubed. Again this rule may apply to Wave a in a corrective phase.

IT (if the Third wave is being corrected)

$$IT_{price} = Z_{price} + (Y_{price} - Z_{price}) \times 1.618^1$$

IF (if the First wave is being corrected)

$$IF_{price} = Z_{price} + (Y_{price} - Z_{price}) \times 1.618^2$$

IX (if the First wave correction extends)

$$IX_{price} = Z_{price} + (Y_{price} - Z_{price}) \times 1.618^3$$

The Rule of Three

The simplest of the forecasting calculations is the Rule of Three, which simply multiplies the magnitude of Wave 1 by three and adds it back to the beginning of Wave 1, which by definition, is an impulse wave. The market is not linear but curved or exponential. As a result, to perform this function, the calculation must be reduced to a logarithmic basis *prior to* multiplying by three, as shown.

$$\text{Rule of Three Target} = e^{[\ln X + 3 \times (\ln Y - \ln X)]}$$

Applying the Rules

In this section, we will examine some examples of situations which would call for us to choose utilization of one of the extension rules over the others based on market conditions.

Shorter Than Rule

If we have a situation such that Wave 1 and Wave 3 are complete, the forecaster will then focus on predicting the extent of Wave 5. Let's say, that Wave 1 in a trend is equal to Wave 3 and both have been fairly large impulse moves, then the forecaster should concentrate on determining the characteristics of Wave 5. Wave 3 is never the shortest wave and is, in fact, generally the longest. Thus, if Wave 1 is equal to Wave 3, which is never the shortest, then it stands to reason that Wave 1 is not the shortest either. Now the shorter than rule can be

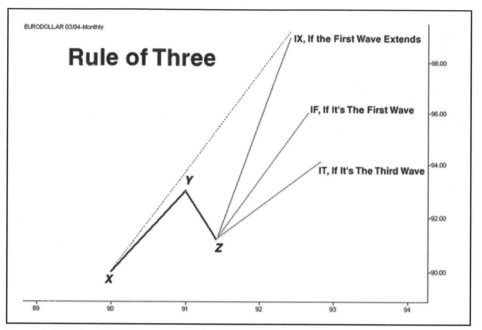

Figure 3–3 IT, IF, and IX Rules and the Rule of Three

used to arrive at a price that is 0.618 times the difference in price between the beginning of Wave 2 and the beginning of Wave 1 added to the price at the end of Wave 2. This could be called a "0.618 extension."

This is a situation in which the smaller than rule may be used. Point X is \$204.90, point Y at the top of Wave 3 is \$243.90, and point Z at the bottom of the correction of Wave 4 is \$226.75.

The length of Wave 3 is Y minus X or \$243.90 minus \$204.90 to equal \$39.00. Multiplied by 0.618, the length of Wave 5 would equal 24.102. This is added to point Z to arrive at an expected price of \$250.85. In actuality, the move ended just 45 cents below this area at \$250.40.

$$\text{Wave 1} = \$218.90 - \$183.90 = \$35.00$$

$$\text{Wave 3} = \$243.90 - \$204.90 = \$39.00$$

$$X_{\text{Wave 3}} = \$204.90,\ Y_{\text{Wave 3}} = \$243.90,\ Z_{\text{Wave 3}} = \$226.75,\ Y_{\text{Wave 3}} - X_{\text{Wave 3}} = \$39.$$

$$\text{Wave 5 expectation} = \$226.75 + (0.618 \times 39) =$$
$$\$226.75 + \$24.1 = \$250.85$$

$$\text{Actual} = \$250.40$$

Figure 3–4 June 1986 S&P Daily: Shorter than Rule

Another time when the smaller than rule may apply is if Wave 1 is approximately equal to 0.618 of Wave 3, Wave 3 is the largest wave, and the two other impulse move waves are close to the same size, it is reasonable to believe that Wave 5 would equal Wave 1 and, thus, would be equal to 0.618 multiplied by Wave 3.

The June 1986 S&P daily chart, illustrated in Figure 3–4, demonstrates a situation where Waves 1 and 3 are approximately the same size. Using the logic described above, it can be expected that Wave 5 will probably be shorter than both preceding impulse moves.

Equal To Rule

In a situation in which Wave 1 is unusually small and Wave 3 has been a fairly large impulse move, it is unlikely that Wave 5 will also be a dwarf or small wave similar to Wave 1. We know that two waves are generally equal, so we can assume that Wave 5 will probably be equal to Wave 3, unless Wave 5 extends, in which case it will be longer. (The equal to rule also applies to clean *abc* corrections.)

Figure 3–5 illustrates how the equal to rule works. The figure is an intraday chart of February 1995 natural gas that demonstrates the *a* and *b* of an *abc* correction, in which X equals $1.52, Y equals $1.58, and Z equals $1.55. In this case, *c* is first expected to be equal to *a*. The difference between $1.58 and $1.52, which is $0.06, is added to the $1.55, for an expectation of $1.61. The actual completion of the move was $1.62.

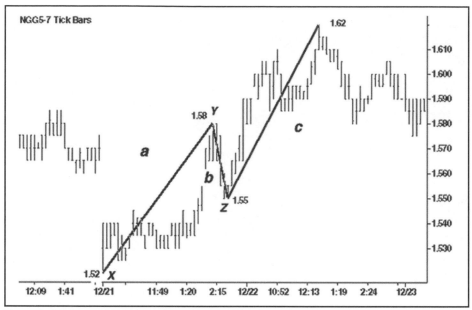

Figure 3–5 February 1995 Natural Gas: Equal to Rule (*c = a*)

$$\$1.58 - \$1.52 = a = 6 \text{ cents}$$

$$\$1.55 + .\$06 = \$1.61$$

$$\text{Actual} = 1.62$$

Longer Than Rule

If Wave 1 is complete and Wave 3, currently in progress, is already longer than Wave 1 and continues to grow, the longer than rule is employed. The length of Wave 1 is multiplied by 1.618 to see where the end of Wave 3 will be. (This also works in *abc* correction patterns. If Wave *c* is already longer than Wave *a*, it likely will extend to [(*Y* − *X*) 1.618 + *Z*].

   Figure 3–6 shows completed Waves 1 and 2. Point *X* equals $16.25, point *Y* equals $15.86, and point *Z* equals $16.04. Point *Y* minus point *X* equals a negative $0.39. We know we are looking at a downward move, since point *Y* minus point *X* is a negative number. Again, as soon as either Wave 3 exceeds the requirements for being equal to Wave 1 or Wave *c* exceeds the requirements of being equal to Wave *a*, the longer than rule applies. As soon as price falls below 15.65 or $16.04 minus $0.39, the longer than rule applies.

$$L = 1.618\,(Y - X) + Z, \text{ so } L =$$
$$1.618\,(-\$0.39) + \$16.04 = \$15.41.$$

The actual low of Wave 3 was $15.40.

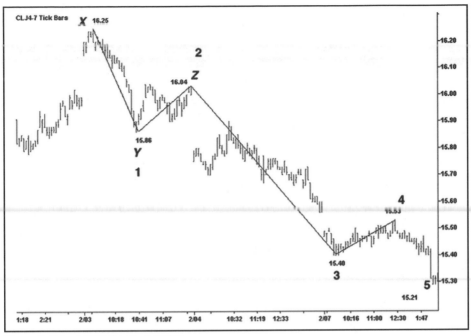

Figure 3–6 April 1994 Crude, Intraday

IT, IF, and IX Rules

The IT, IF, and IX rules are:

IT — **If** it is the **T**hird, or c, wave

IF — **If** it is the **F**irst, or a, wave

IX — **If** it is the first, or a wave, e**X**tended

As far as corrective extensions are concerned, the IT, IF, and IX relationships are the most likely to occur. There are times when, for example, the IF rule works with Wave 3. My recommendation is to calculate the IT, IF, and IX rules for both the first and third wave corrections, as applicable, and with a view to addressing specific problems as they arise.

The Rule of Three

The Rule of Three can be used *anytime* Wave 1 has been identified. Figure 3–7 is a good example of the Rule of Three used on Wave 1 of a bull market move in natural gas that occurred in 1993. The May contract reached a high of $2.80, after which the market made a severe correction.

$$X = \$1.50, Y = \$1.85$$

$$\ln(\$1.85) - \ln(\$1.51) = \$0.615 - \$0.412 = \$0.203$$

$$\$0.203 \times 3 = \$0.609$$

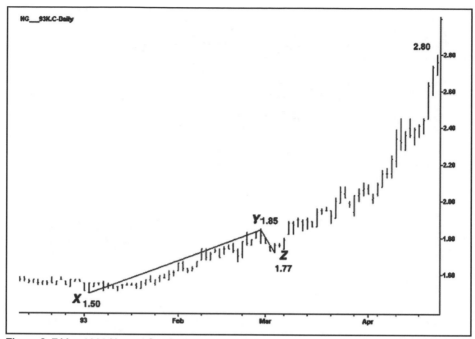

Figure 3–7 May 1993 Natural Gas Daily in Bull Market

$$\$0.609 \ + \ \ln(\$1.51) \ = \ \$0.609 \ + \ \$0.412 \ = \ \$1.021$$

$$\exp(\$1.021) \ = \ \$2.776$$

$$\text{Actual} \ = \ \$2.80$$

Here a logarithmic extension should be used because there has been a fairly large market move, where X equals $1.50 and Y equals $1.85. The logarithmic move of $1.85 minus $1.51 is ln(1.85) minus ln(1.51), or 0.615 minus 0.412, for a difference of 0.203. That number is multiplied by 3 and added to the log of 1.51 (.609 + .615 = 1.224), and the exponential of the result is used.

The resulting expected target is $2.776. The actual market high was $2.80.

RETRACEMENTS

All markets correct themselves and usually retrace previous moves by certain predictable percentages. In a weak trend in which the market lacks conviction, many traders will take a profit after a small move, while others will be quick to reverse positions, causing a deep retracement. In a strong market, many traders will hold their positions, while others will be less likely to take opposing positions, thus causing a more shallow correction.

The most commonly used retracement percentages are 38, 50, and 62. The markets in general seem to "rebound" to these levels. Retracements of 21 and 89 percent also occur too often to be ignored, indicating that the initial force was either very strong or very weak. The larger the force, the smaller the retracement.

A retracement is calculated by multiplying the value from the beginning of an impulse wave to the beginning of a corrective wave (i.e., X minus Y) by the retracement fraction (0.38, 0.50, etc.) and adding the result to the value of the beginning of the corrective wave (i.e., Z).

In a rising market, the value (X minus Y) will be negative, indicating a move down, against the trend, to a retracement target lower than Y. In a falling market, X minus Y will be positive, indicating a move up, against the trend to a retracement target higher than Y.

Thus the following formula need not be modified for rising or falling markets.

$$\text{Retracement Target } Z = Y + [\text{Retrace \%} \times (X - Y)]$$

In strong trends, the 21 percent retracement may dominate, especially when the commitment to the trending direction is so strong that attempts at correction basically fail at about the 21 percent level. The 89 percent retracements are common in situations in which trends are relatively weak. Wave 1 corrections in a market in which the trend has not yet caught fire are also very steep, as are corrections that occur over short time-frames in which more erratic behavior is evident.

Corrections will retrace to various levels, as shown in Figure 3–8 indicating varying retracements of one correction based on various pivot points of the move down. The 50 percent retracement of the entire move, the 62 percent retracement of the second leg of the move, and the 89 percent retracement of the final leg of the move can all be identified. All are confluent in the area of $1.675. The actual high is a correction to $1.66. This is an excellent example of confluence.

$$X_1 = 50\% \text{ retrace from \$1.91 to \$1.44} =$$
$$\$1.44 + 0.5 (\$1.91 - \$1.44) = \$1.675$$

$$X_2 = 62\% \text{ retrace from \$1.832 to \$1.44} =$$
$$\$1.44 + 0.62 (\$1.832 - \$1.44) = \$1.683$$

$$X_3 = 89\% \text{ retrace from \$1.695 to \$1.44} =$$
$$\$1.44 + 0.89 (\$1.695 - \$1.44) = \$1.667$$

$$\text{Average expectation} = \$1.675$$

$$\text{Actual} = \$1.66$$

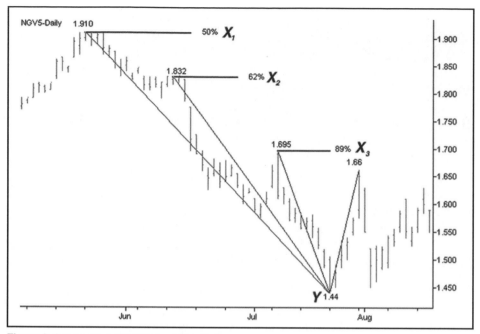

Figure 3–8 November 1995 Natural Gas Daily

THE FORECASTING GRID

A table or grid can be created for every set of three prices (points X, Y, and Z) of the resulting projections and retracements of these levels. This is exactly what I do in order to prepare my weekly forecasts. For every contract, on a weekly basis, there are normally about 30 sets of points X, Y, and Z to calculate. Eventually, 50 or 60 sets of weekly and daily waves can be built.

Forecasting Grid

	1	2	3	4
a	X			
b	Y	Z retraces % of XY		
c	Z	S	E	L
d	21%	S	E	L
e	38%	S	E	L
f	50%	S	E	L
g	62%	S	E	L
h	89%	S	E	L
i	IT	IF	IX	Rule of 3

Forecasting Grid Legend

Column 1, a, b, and c	The X, Y, and Z prices
Column 2, b	The percentage of XY, which Z retraces
Columns 2, 3, and 4 c	The shorter than, equal to, and longer than extensions of the XYZ set
Column 1, d through h	The 21, 38, 50, 62, and 89 % retracements of XY to be used in cases in which Z is not yet known
Columns 2, 3, and 4, d through h	The shorter than, equal to and longer than extensions of the XY and the % retrace value set, to be used in cases in which Z is not yet known
Columns 1, 2, and 3 I	The IT, IF, and IX extensions of the YZ pair of prices
Column 4 I	The XY length multiplied by 3 on a log basis and added to X

The two hypothetical Eurodollar charts in Figures 3–2 and 3–3 should be referred to when discussing how to calculate extensions, as follows:

The XYZ set is defined as $X = 90$, $Y = 93$ and $Z = 91.14$.

Filling in the forecasting grid with these values yields the following results:

	1	2	3	4
a	90			
b	93	62%		
c	91.14	92.99	94.14	95.99
i	94.15	96.01	99.02	99.30

Column 2, cell b, indicates that price Z is a 62 percent retracement. Confluence can be identified around 94.15, 96.00, and 99.

Assuming that point X constitutes the origin of this move and is, therefore, the origin of Wave 1, it can be postulated that the entire move will extend to about $99, which corresponds to the Rule of Three. It can be predicted that the end of Wave 3 might be around 96 but that it will meet major resistance, such as the Wave 4 correction of Wave 3 (each impulse wave breaks down into five smaller waves) at about $94.

In sum, the incorporation of forecasting techniques into the trading game plan allows for a highly accurate analysis of market direction. It takes hard work and proper application of the right tools, but the payoff potential is tremendous.

Using Chart Formations In Forecasting

Traditional geometric chart formations were originally identified in early technical literature, a subject sometimes referred to as charting, and analysts who rely heavily on these techniques are often called chartists. There are two major subcategories of geometric chart formations: reversal and continuation patterns.

The term *reversal pattern* can be slightly confusing. These patterns indicate that the existing trend is unlikely to continue; they do not necessarily indicate a reversal. The trend could simply end, with prices meandering sideways for a while. Reversal patterns might be more aptly called "noncontinuation" patterns and include such formations as *spike tops, v-bottoms, double tops and bottoms, head and shoulders,* and *symmetrical triangles.*

Continuation patterns, as the name implies, indicate that an existing trend is likely to continue. These patterns include formations such as *wedges*, *pennants,* and *flags*.

REVERSAL PATTERNS

Spike Tops and V-Bottoms

The spike top and its inverse, the spike or V-bottom, is indicative of a panic rush to buy or sell, generally due either to greed or fear or a combination of the two. The panic pushes prices to an extreme when, in fact, the overriding market momentum is in the opposite direction.

Sugar in late 1975 exhibited such a spike formation (see Figure 3A–1). In a topping formation, buyers rushed into the market in fear, either panicked to cover a losing short position or afraid that sugar would disappear forever. The sellers delayed liquidating their positions because of greed, that is they hoped the price would continue rising until the market was so overdone to the upside that it crashed of its own weight.

As is often the case with geometric formations, the spike was accompanied by a traditional bar reversal pattern, in this case an *island reversal*. In an uptrend, an island reversal is defined as a pattern in which a market gaps higher and then follows a bar that gaps to the downside, leaving a lone bar or "island" above the market. The reverse is true at a market bottom. As a general rule, the bar sitting above the market will open and close in the lower half of the bar's range, while at a bottom, the open and close will be in the upper half of the bar's range.

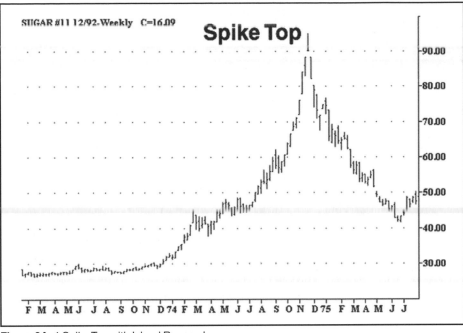

Figure 3A–1 Spike Top with Island Reversal

Double Tops and Bottoms

Double tops and bottoms are similar to the spike top or bottom. This formation is characterized by an "M" formation at market tops, or a "W" formation at market bottoms (see Figure 3A–2). The difference is that the bulls (in an up-market) or bears (in a down-market) make a second attempt to push the market in their direction, but fail.

Triple tops or bottoms can also occur, but are rare.

Head and Shoulders

The head and shoulders formation is comprised of a left shoulder, which, in an up-market, is a new high followed by a head that is a higher high, followed by a right shoulder or lower high. The support line below the head and shoulders formation is called the neckline (see Figure 3A–3).

The right shoulder is a rally that fails to reach the height of the head, meaning that the attempt at a new high has failed. This should occur on a decrease in volume. The inverse is true for the formation at the bottom of the market, which is called an inverse head and shoulders (see Figure 3A–4).

Head and shoulder formations can be used to forecast price. Two approaches, equally valid, may be used. Figure 3A–5 illustrates both techniques, resulting in similar forecasts, which were quite accurate.

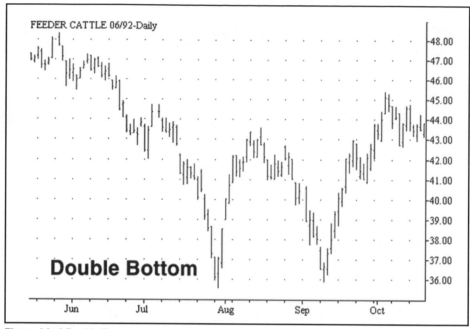

Figure 3A–2 Double Bottom

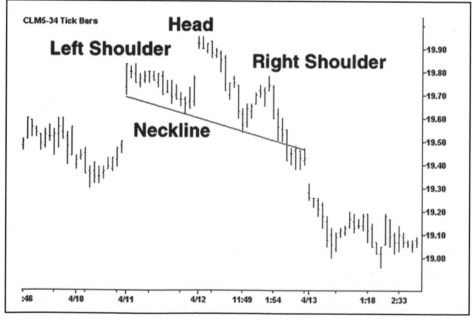

Figure 3A–3 Head and Shoulders Pattern

The first technique requires that the distance from the peak of the head to the neckline be measured and that value deducted from the neckline. The resultant value, is the target price. The formula is:

Neckline – (Peak of Head – Neckline) = Target 1

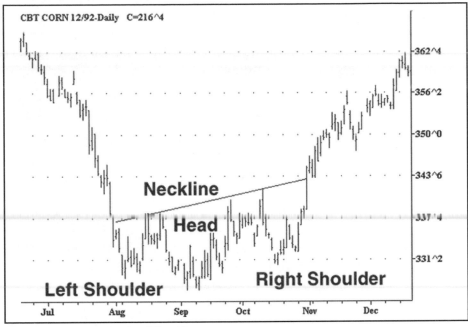

Figure 3A–4 Inverse Head and Shoulder

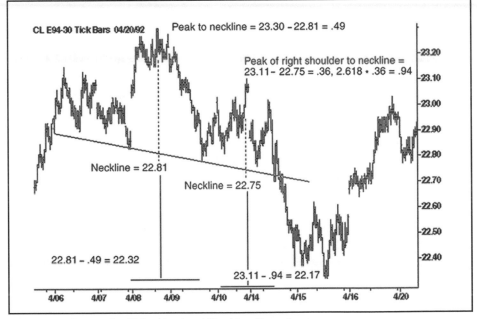

Figure 3A–5 Forecasting Using Head and Shoulders Formations

In the example in Figure 3A–5, this would result in a target of 22.32 as shown:

$$22.81 - (23.30 - 22.81) = 22.81 - .49 = 22.32$$

The second technique measures from the peak of the right shoulder to the neckline, multiplies this value by 2.618 (a Fibonacci ratio), and deducts this value from the peak of the right shoulder. This is the second "target" price. The formula is:

Peak of Right Shoulder – [(Peak of Right Shoulder – Neckline) × 2.618]
= Target 2

This results, as shown below, in a target of 22.17:

23.11 – [(23.11 – 22.75) × 2.618] = 23.11 – (.36 × 2.618) =
23.11 – .94 = 22.17

In this example, the first technique proved to be more accurate as the market hit a low of exactly $22.32. It is often the case that target one will be exceeded and target two will be more accurate.

Symmetrical Triangle

The symmetrical triangle is a large topping formation often seen after a sustained bull market. However, it is characterized by lower highs and higher lows in a contracting pattern (see Figure 3A–6).

The symmetrical triangle is generated by a high degree of uncertainty in the market. Rather than the bulls and bears fighting it out in one major battle (as in the spike), small skirmishes take place be-

Figure 3A–6 Symmetrical Triangle

tween some buyers and sellers, while others wait on the sidelines for a resolution.

Coils or Springs

A coil, also called a spring, is a formation that looks similar to a symmetrical triangle. One difference is that symmetrical triangles usually form fairly large structures, while coils can be either small or large. Another difference is that they can take place in either bull or bear markets.

A coil usually forms during a period of market uncertainty and, thus, projects a market move that could turn in either direction. In other words, it can be either a continuation or a reversal pattern. In any case, a market move using a coil is projected by measuring the maximum distance on the wide part of the coil and projecting up or down from the apex. This technique is illustrated in Figure 3A–7.

$$\text{Apex} - \text{Width of Coil} = \text{Target}$$

$$49.45 - (49.80 - 48.70) = 49.45 - 1.10 = 49.35$$

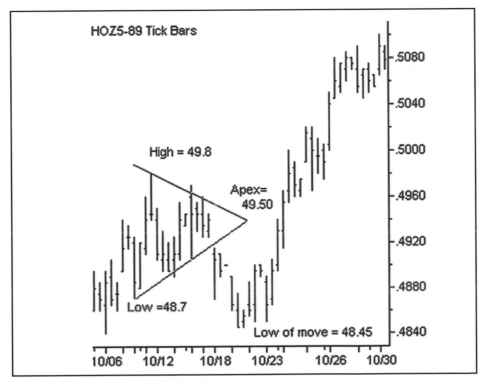

Figure 3A–7 Forecasting Using Coils or Springs

In this case, the width of the coil is 1.10 cents. The width subtracted from the apex projects a target of 48.35, which was met within
1/10 of a cent.

CONTINUATION PATTERNS

The patterns noted are generally reversal patterns, with the exception of coils, which can also be continuation patterns. Other examples
of continuation patterns include flags, pennants, and wedges (see Figure 3A–8) and are merely pauses or shallow corrections against the
trend. The market should break out of these patterns in the direction of the trend.

Measuring Gaps

Certain gaps can also signal the continuation of a trend. Furthermore,
they can be used to forecast the magnitude of a price move. This type
of gap, known as a midpoint or measuring gap, will occur in the
middle of a market move. To project a target in an upmove, the price
is measured from the low of the move to the bottom of the gap and
this number is added to the top of the gap to result in a minimum

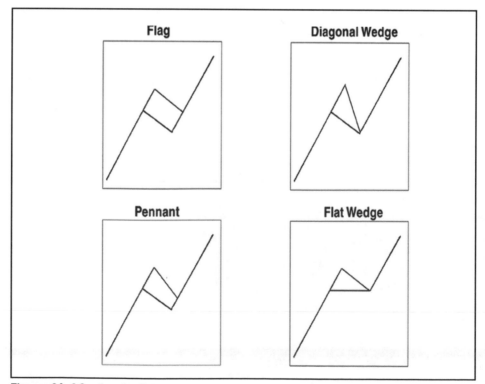

Figures 3A–8 Continuation Patterns

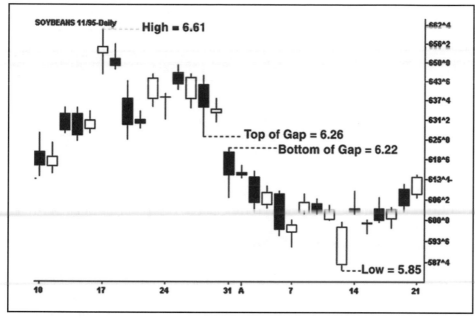

Figure 3A–9 Measuring Gap

target the market can be expected to reach. The reverse is true for a downmove, as shown in Figure 3A–9.

In this case, the distance from the high to the top of the gap is 35 cents ($6.61 minus $6.26 equals 0.35). This number, subtracted from the bottom of the gap, $6.22, generates a target of $5.87. The market exceeded this target by two cents, reaching a low of $5.85.

CHAPTER 4

Improving the Probability of Success with Time Diversification

The concept of minimizing the inherent risk in trading by using diversity has become standard wisdom among traders since Richard Donchian advocated the idea in the December, 1974 issue of *Commodities* magazine. Most traders implement the idea by trading a portfolio of commodities or instruments. However, if a trader is limited to trading a single commodity, how can this principle be applied? The answer is to diversify using multiple levels of *time*.

In order to understand multiple time-frame techniques, a good understanding of two basic concepts is required: multiple time-frames and diversification using time.

Multiple time-frame techniques require that *multiple* (never less than two) time-frames be used in trading. For example, in a long-term bull market, the probabilities are that long trades, in general, will be more successful than short trades. In a long-term bear market, the probability is that short trades will be more successful than long trades. Thus, the longer-term direction of the market can be used to influence trade decisions. A multiple time-frame technique can help to filter trades based on the longer-term direction. Some new types of multiple time-frame techniques, when coupled with a computer's capability and speed, can provide a whole new way to examine longer-term data.

Diversification is accomplished by what I call "scaling-up" and "scaling-down" in time. Diversification is a way of managing risk, which is logically related to time. The longer a position is held, the more the market can move and, thus, the greater the potential to lose money. If a trade is taken in a short time-frame, e.g., in 15-minute bars, the amount of money that could be lost on the trade is related to the risk associated with the range of the 15-minute bar. If the 15-minute trades make money, eventually a signal would be received and the trade taken on a 30-minute bar. This would carry commensurate additional risk, but the risk would be buffered by the profit on the earlier position. If successful, eventually a signal would be received to move up to a 60-minute bar, a 90-minute bar, and so on, risking more but being buffered by the profit on the earlier positions and allowing, perhaps, for greater profit with each incremental increase in the time-frame.

In actual practice, a trader would not use so many multiple increments. The idea, however, is that a successful trade in a short time-frame bar will offer a profit in a position to buffer the level of risk in a medium time-frame bar. If there is a profit in the medium time-frame, a buffer against the risk will be taken in an even longer time-frame bar, and so on. This is the concept of "scaling-up" to higher or longer-term time frames.

"Dropping-down" in time involves taking signals from very short-term price movement in order to improve entries. A short-term pull-back or retracement often follows after an initial entry signal is generated. With careful observation, this technique can provide an opportunity to enter the market at a slightly more favorable level. At the very least, it can compensate for the normal execution losses (slippage) and brokerage commissions that decrease trading profits.

SCREENING TRADES

The market is fractally symmetrical and multilayered. Continuing the analogy of the Russian dolls discussed in Chapter 2, each doll can be thought of as an Elliott Wave at increasingly smaller market levels. The tick level is the equivalent of the smallest doll, which cannot be further reduced. Likewise, larger and larger dolls are added until they simply become too big to manage. Larger and larger wave patterns can be seen until they simply involve time-frames that are too large to be meaningful, e.g., if the time-frame is outside the normal market cycle lengths or carries too high a risk even with scale-up techniques.

The objective is to find the optimal combination of dolls, or levels of the market, that will provide the most effective analysis of the market's actions. For example, as noted on the daily chart in the lower half of Figure 4–1 several buy signals occurred in 1991. The run-ups end before they influence the weekly chart to any great extent. The larger or screen time-frame works as an effective screening mechanism for determining which actions are actually noise on the shorter time-frame chart. Generally, this screen time-frame should be three to five times the monitor time-frame.

Screening Using Trending Filters

To understand the screening methodology, we can begin with a simple application, screening a moving average crossover in the shorter-term with a moving average crossover in a longer-term. The rules for this system are:

1. If, in the longer time-frame, the fast (shorter) moving average is *above* the slow moving average, only *long* trades are permissioned in the shorter time-frame.

2. If, in the longer time-frame, the fast (shorter) moving average is *below* the slow moving average, only *short* trades are permissioned in the shorter time-frame.

The word permissioned here has a slightly different connotation than the word "allowed." Just as a child knows he is allowed to leave the table after he receives permission, the market will *allow* a trader to do anything he wants, including making mistakes and losing money. The word permission implies that an authority, be it an individual, a machine, or a set of rules, has agreed that certain conditions have been met and has given permission for the trader to take certain actions.

Figure 4–1 is a soybean continuation chart that covers a portion of market activity from the summer of 1991 to the summer of 1992. The top of the chart illustrates weekly (or longer-term) normalized data, and the bottom chart indicates daily (or shorter-term) normalized continuation data. Both subgraphs show 10-period and 21-period simple moving averages. The fast moving average (10-pe-

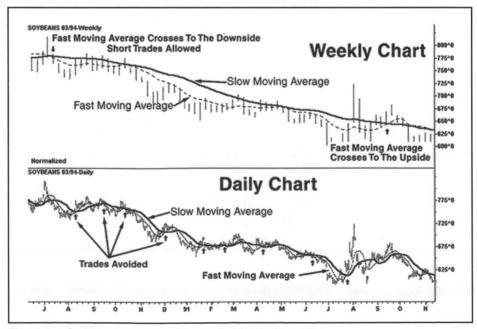

Figure 4–1 Soybean Continuation Chart, July 1990 to June 1991

riod) is represented by the dotted line; the slow (21-day moving average) is represented by the solid line.

On the weekly chart, the fast moving average crosses to the downside in August, 1991 and stays below the slow moving average until approximately September of the following year. During this period, only short trades would be permissioned on the daily chart, thus avoiding many whipsaw trades shown by the moving average crossovers and up-arrows on the bottom chart.

No system is perfect. All screening systems allow losing trades from time to time, and all such systems occasionally screen out winning trades. The objective is not perfection, which is impossible, but rather profitable traders.

Figure 4–2 illustrates that the same approach can be used for shorter-term data. This chart shows July 1994 crude oil. The top chart is a 65-minute chart, a chart that constitutes 1/5 of the day session for crude oil. The bottom chart is approximately 1/3 that length.

On June 8, 1994 the fast moving average crosses above the slow moving average on the 65-minute chart and remains above it for the life of the chart, ending in June. Two crosses to the downside of the fast moving average are shown on the shorter-term chart. Using the longer time-frame as a screen eliminated both short-term whipsaw trades.

Figure 4–3, a natural gas weekly and daily continuation chart, illustrates trades for all of 1992 and part of 1993. Part of the diffi-

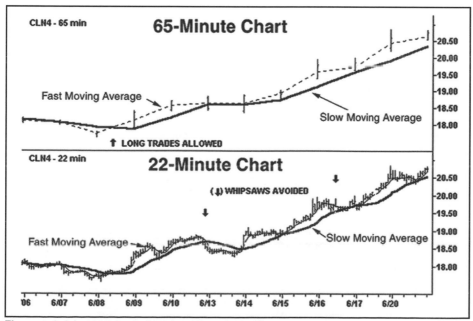

Figure 4–2 July 1994 Crude Intraday, 65- and 22-minute

culty in using a longer-term filter is the lag in receiving permission to go long or short from the longer time-frame. The up-trend on this chart, beginning in late March on the daily screen, was not permissioned until May on the longer, weekly chart. Likewise, the down-trend and subsequent up-trend are permissioned late by the long-term screen. Trending indicators, by definition, are lagging indicators. Therefore, using trending indicators exaggerates the lag time.

Trending indicators are also prone to whipsaws. In markets that are oscillating or in which the trend duration is relatively short, permission can be gained constantly *after* signals are generated. This is true for all time-frames in which trending indicators are used.

The first arrow on the left of the daily chart in Figure 4–3 shows a short signal in early December 1991. That short signal is not permissioned on the upper chart until the middle of January. In 1992, there is a good long trade signal in late February and another in the middle of April. Long trades are not permissioned until early May. Later that year, after the market run-up is over, there is a good trade. This time the short trade signal was generated around November 19, and short trades were not permissioned until Christmas time. In early 1993, there was a good long trade in the middle of February, followed by a pullback and another long trade in early March. Neither trade was permissioned long until the middle of

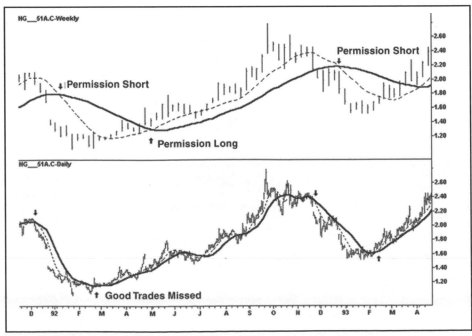

Figure 4–3 Natural Gas 1992 to 1993 with Trend Filter

April. Thus, six good trading opportunities would have been missed by using this trending filter permissioning system.

Screening Using Momentum Filters

More sensitive screening mechanisms can be provided by using momentum rather than trending filters. Using the well known Slow Stochastic study as a screen helps to illustrate this. From time to time, some sacrifices will be experienced in a moderately higher level of whipsaws. In general, however, results will be superior, as shown in Figure 4–4. This chart displays the same data as the trending indicator (see Figure 4–3) but uses a Slow Stochastic filter. (For information about calculating the Stochastic, see Chapter 4 Appendix, "The Traditional Stochastic Indicator.")

The top chart is a weekly nine-period stochastic. The moving averages on the bottom daily chart are repeated from Figure 4–3. The arrows show all the good trades taken. The Xs show a missed good trade in July of 1992 and a whipsaw trade taken in October. Overall, however, the results from the five successful trades outweigh the small losses incurred by missing the July up-move and taking the small whipsaw trade in October.

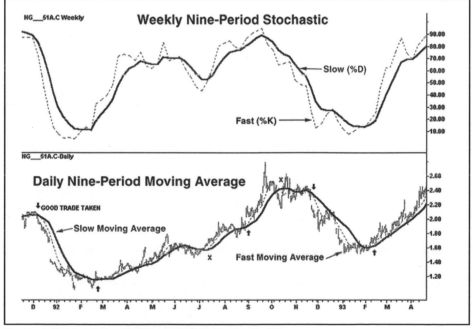

Figure 4–4 Natural Gas 1992 to 1993 with Stochastic Filter

Bar Numbering Protocol

When discussing bars in trading algorithms, formulae, and systems, it is customary to count backwards from the current day's bar. The most recent bar (e.g., today's bar on a daily chart) is bar *zero*. The *preceding* bar (the bar directly to the *left* of the most recent bar) is bar 1. The next preceding bar (the third bar back from the most recent bar) is bar 2. The numbers are generally shown in brackets, [ ], to differentiate them from parentheses, ( ), which usually contain formulae or algorithms.

Thus, if there are five daily bars (see Figure 4–5) used in a formula, they would be bar zero (today), bar one (yesterday), bar two (two days ago), bar three (three days ago), and bar four (four days ago). To take this one step further, there are n number of bars in a formula, which would be bar *zero* through bar $n - 1$, the most recent bar in the previous time segment. This conventional counting system is the most practical for purposes of trading algorithms because various formulae employ differing numbers of data points to calculate the result. (Because most of us are used to counting from left to right rather than from right to left, the system can feel a bit awkward at first.)

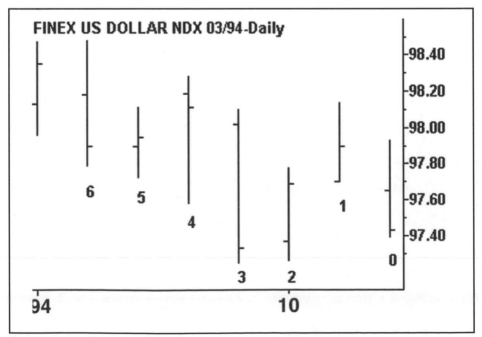

Figure 4–5 Bar Numbering Protocol

THE KASE PERMISSION STOCHASTIC:
REDEFINING TIME

Though the Stochastic generates more sensitive signals than a trending indicator, such as a moving average, if a trader wants to use a time-frame that is, for instance, five time-frames higher than the shorter (monitor) time-frame, he may have to wait for the completion of four additional bars *after* receiving a signal before the permitting time-frame kicks in with the permissioning signal.

For example, a trader who has been trading based on a daily bar is using a weekly bar to screen his trade. He has exited a short position the previous Friday and is looking for the market to turn to the upside. On Monday, just prior to the close, he checks his daily bar and receives what he believes to be a good buy signal. He must now wait until the close on Friday for the weekly bar to give him a signal regarding the higher time-frame Stochastic status. In the case of a shorter-term trader, the trader may receive a signal 10 minutes into a 50-minute time period and must wait for 40 additional minutes for the 50-minute screen to give a permissioning signal. Most traders lack the patience to wait for permissioning signals under these circumstances.

The solution is to redefine the longer time-frame. Who says that a week must end on Friday? A week can be *any* five consecutive trading days. Therefore, on a given Monday, a week would have started the previous Tuesday and ended on that given Monday. On Tuesday, a week begins on the previous Wednesday, and so on.

If trading 10-minute bars and screening 10-minute bars with 50-minute bars, a trader can define the 50-minute screening time-frame as the 50-minutes up to and including the completion of the current 10-minute bar. Thus, he has a moving, higher time-frame screen or window that updates at the completion of every bar. This is the best compromise between conservatism (by screening all trades in a higher time-frame) and time sensitivity (by using the momentum filter that updates at the end of every bar). The trader would not have been excessively conservative in screening and would have taken the most aggressive (justifiable) approach.

Synthetic bars allow this transformation of the screening time-frame so that the time-frame can be updated at the end of every bar. These bars *synthesize* what the bar would look like over the past specified number of periods.

A traditional week ends on Friday. Therefore, the open of the week is Monday's open. The high of the week is the highest trade that takes place between Monday and Friday, and the low of the week is the lowest trade that takes place between Monday and Friday. The close of the week is simply Friday's close.

If today is Wednesday and the market has closed, then the open of this week was the open of the previous Thursday. The high of the week was the highest trade between the previous Thursday and today, Wednesday, and the lowest trade between the previous Thursday and today constitutes the low. Today's (Wednesday's) close is the close of the week. Tomorrow (Thursday), the previous Friday's open will be the open of the week. The highest trade between the previous Friday and Thursday will be the high of the week, and the lowest trade between the previous Friday and Thursday will be the low of the week; Thursday's close will be the close of the week, and so on. The same procedure applies for any time-frame combination, be it 10- and 50-minute bars, five- and 25-minute bars, etc.

The procedure used to calculate the open, high, low, and close of synthetic bars is outlined in the sidebar on the following page. Once the synthetic bar open, high, low, and close are calculated, all that is required to create synthetic indicators is to substitute the synthetic open, high, low, and close for the normal open, high, low, and close generally included in algorithms. The number sequencing and counting can then be adjusted accordingly. Thus, a synthetic Stochastic can be calculated and the synthetic Stochastic can be smoothed several times to remove some of the "wiggles" that are generated when the indicator updates every day rather than every five bars.

For example, if calculating a nine-period Stochastic on a synthetic weekly bar, the trader will need five times nine (i.e., 45 daily bars) plus one for the previous close, or 46. Thus, if he wishes to count the numbers of bars back for various formulae, instead of $x + 1$, he will need $(x \times n) + 1$. Thus, for the previous close he would use close [5] (the most recent close of the previous segment) instead of using yesterday's close, or close [1]. If he wanted to look at the close of two segments back, he would look at close [10] rather than close [2], and so on.

These values can be substituted into the formula for the Stochastic with the additional smoothing step to reduce some of the erratic waves created from the sensitive nature of this indicator. This provides a time-frame that updates at the end of every bar. The trader can use the longer-term screening time-frame without having to wait for completion of additional bars.

FORMING SYNTHETIC BARS

1. n = number of bars to merge, e.g., n = 5 to convert a daily into a weekly synthetic bar

2. Synthetic high = max (H [0] to H [$n - 1$]);
    The maximum high of bars [0], [1], [2], [3], and [4].

3. Synthetic low = min (L [0] to L [$n - 1$]);
    The minimum low of bars [0], [1], [2], [3], and [4].

4. Synthetic open = open [$n - 1$] ;
    The open five days back would be the open of bar [4].

5. Synthetic close = close [0] ;
    The close of n bars would be the close of bar [0] or the most current bar.

6. Synthetic previous close = close [n];
    The close of the previous segment would be the close of bar [5] or the close six days back.

7. Number of bars for total length of longer term indicators = $x \times n$ (where x is the length or periodicity of the longer term indicator).

    For example, to get nine weekly bars, x = 9. Then, $x \times n = 9 \times 5 = 45$ bars.

8. For number of bars back, [x] is changed to [$x \times n$] + 1, where x = any periodicity input into the indicator.

    As with item 7, above, the number of bars back to count would be $(9 \times 5) + 1 = 46$ bars.

    The values above in any normal formula for indicators are substituted and smoothed as necessary.

    In this example, n is the number of bars to merge. If n = 5, this creates a weekly synthetic bar from daily information. If a 15-minute bar is converted into an hourly bar, n would be set to equal 4. If there are five hours in day and the trader wishes to convert an hourly chart into a weekly chart, n = 25 would be used and so on. Synthetic high is simply the maximum of the high from bar zero to bar [$n - 1$]. Thus, if n = 5, the trader is counting from bar zero to bar four.

    The Synthetic low is similarly calculated as the minimum of this range. The synthetic open is the open of bar [$n - 1$], and the synthetic close is the close of the current bar or bar [0]. With this procedure, the close of the previous bar is not close [1], as it would be with normal bars, but close [n]. In this example, converting daily bar information into a weekly bar, the synthetic previous close is the close of the sixth bar back.

THE KASE PERMISSION STOCHASTIC:
A BETTER SCREEN

Figure 4–6 illustrates the same natural gas daily data series as Figure 4–4, but this time it is accompanied by the weekly Stochastic and the Kase Permission Stochastic.

Kase Permission Stochastic Filters

While there appears to be more noise on the Kase Permission Stochastic, in a general sense, the two charts look relatively similar. The permission-K and the permission-D in the Kase Permission Stochastic, parallel the %K and %D in the traditional Stochastic; the two charts tend to fluctuate together. The Kase Permission Stochastic, though "noisier," has fewer whipsaw crossovers than the traditional, longer time-frame slow Stochastic. Indeed, research indicates that the number of whipsaws are generally reduced by about 80 percent using the Kase Permission Stochastic. If the time around the middle of December, 1993 is carefully examined, a whipsaw crossover will be noted in the regular weekly Stochastic, while the Kase Permission Stochastic does not cross.

My research also indicates that the Kase Permission Stochastic crosses ahead of a normal longer time-frame Stochastic more than 80 percent of the time and usually leads by one or two days. Careful examination of Figure 4–7 demonstrates that in June the Kase Permission Stochastic crossed unusually early (13 days ahead of the normal Stochastic). This occurred because of an unusually

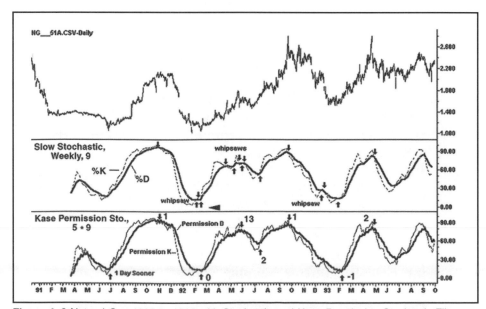

Figure 4–6 Natural Gas 1992 to 1993 with Stochastic and Kase Permission Stochastic Filters

high number of whipsaws, noted earlier in a normal Stochastic. In this case, a normal Stochastic whipsawed up and down a number of times prior to crossing to the downside, while the Kase Permission Stochastic simply generated a normal crossover signal.

Figure 4–7 shows the same contract, first nearby natural gas, with more recent data and similar results.

CONDENSING THE INFORMATION

Using the Kase Permission Stochastic and synthetic bars accelerates the permissioning process as much as possible without compromising the integrity of the process itself. However, a number of improvements are still possible. First, the permissioning process must be more comprehensive than simply permission-K and permission-D crossovers.

Oversold and overbought markets must also be discussed because the terms oversold and overbought can be misleading. Truly overbought or oversold markets are those in which prices have pushed to false extremes, out of line with underlying supply and demand factors in the market. The standard use of the terminology generally denotes periods of time during which momentum indicators, such as the Stochastic and RSI, reach arbitrarily determined high or low *numerical* levels.

Many traders are taught to sell the market when it is overbought and buy the market when it is oversold. The problem with

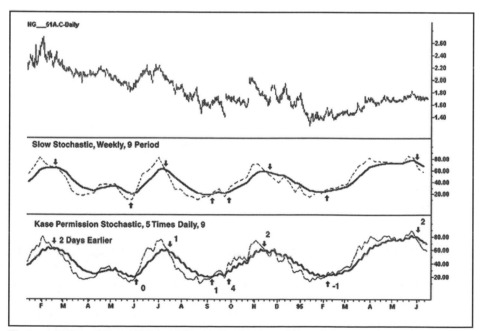

Figure 4–7 Natural Gas 1994 to 1995 with Stochastic and Kase Permission Stochastic Filters

THE KASE PERMISSION SCREEN RULES

Traders can go long when:

1. The Permission Stochastic values are near the top of the chart and close in value.
2. The Permission Stochastic values have been near the bottom of the chart, permission-K is both well above the permission-D and above (or has risen out of) oversold territory.
3. The Permission Stochastic values are both below 85 percent and above 15 percent, and permission-K is above permission-D.

Traders can go short when:

1. The Permission Stochastic values are near the bottom of the chart and close in value.
2. The Permission Stochastic values have been near the top of the chart, permission-K is both well below the permission-D and below (or has fallen out of) overbought territory.
3. The Permission Stochastic values are both below 85 percent and above 15 percent, and permission-K is below permission-D.

Note: The 15 and 85 percentages are commonly used default values for indicating overbought and oversold. Traders can assign their own preferences for these regions, if desired.

this approach is twofold. First, the level of the RSI and Stochastic are directly dependent on the periodicity of the indicator itself. The fewer the number of periods being considered, the more sensitive the indicator and more likely it is to reach one extreme or another. Second, when markets trend, these indicators tend to stay in overbought territory in bull markets and oversold territory in bear markets. In a good bull trending market the Stochastic tends to ride the top of the chart, while in a bear trending market it tends to ride the bottom of the chart.

The concepts of overbought and oversold should be viewed in the light of this reality. Permissioned traders may take long trades when the Permission Stochastic is riding on the top of the chart and when the permission-K and permission-D are close together. They may take short trades when the opposite conditions apply.

It is often important to note when the market falls out of an overbought condition or rises up from an oversold one. Traders are permissioned to take long trades when the market has been in an oversold condition and exhibits a certain amount of divergence, or separation, between the permission-K and permission-D. In other words, traders are permissioned to go long when there is a good differential between the permission-K and permission-D and the permission-K has already rocketed out of the oversold territory. When opposite conditions apply, traders are permissioned to go short. These six permissioning rules are listed in the adjacent sidebar. While these indicators also point out additional, more obscure patterns, the six permissioning rules provide about 80 percent of the value of this indicator.

Condensing more information into a manageable format for the trader has a number of distinct advantages. It helps eliminate judgment errors that often occur when traders are under pressure as well as mathematical errors. Additionally, when the information is presented at a glance in this manner, traders can utilize their time considering trading strategies rather than focusing on fairly simple, but lengthy mathematical calculations.

The condensation of information is most easily represented graphically by a toggle switch. In Figure 4–8 permissioned long is indicated by a solid line histogram and permissioned short is indicated by a dotted line histogram.

When the charts are "live" and on a color screen, permissioned long and permissioned short signals can be represented with different colors rather than dotted and solid lines. The stripes or color bands can also be superimposed on the same chart on which the data is being displayed. Color-coding the backdrop of the data chart to

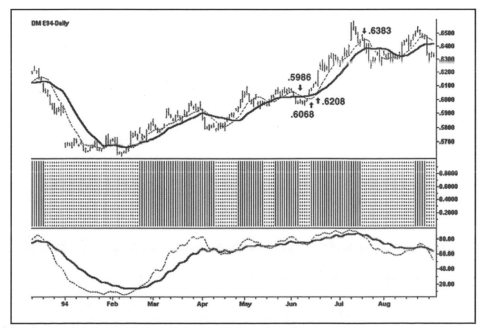

Figure 4–8 DMark Daily with Kase Permission Screen and Stochastic

show permission long and permission short further reduces the level of interpretation required.

KASE WARNING SIGNS

Some situations do not particularly lend themselves to linear algebra. One such phenomenon is called the roll-over effect. This pattern takes place when a spiking or peaking type of market occurs and the permission-K is high, as in the case of an overbought market. Conversely, this also happens when the permission-K is low, showing V-bottom type activity, as in the case of an oversold market. After this point, the permission-K rolls over, with a wide difference between the permission-K and the permission-D crossing.

Because this type of formation is difficult to program, compromises are required in describing this phenomenon (such as deciding the difference between two lines, the height of the permission-K, and the degree to which the permission-K accelerates either downward or upward). Therefore, this phenomenon is best represented as a warning and is represented in its own display. If the warning pertains to shorts, the chart symbol (a cross or dot) appears below the bars; if the warning pertains to longs, the chart symbol appears above the bars. This is shown in the DMark daily chart in Figure 4-9. The chart spans all of

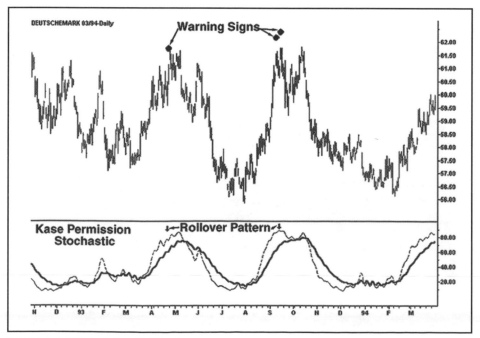

Figure 4–9 DMark Daily with Warnings

1993 and a few months before and after. The formation can be seen by looking at the Stochastic and the areas to which the arrows are pointing.

Once the warning is triggered, the trader may look at the Kase Permission Stochastic itself and make a judgement call as to the quality of the formation. The warning eliminates the need for a trader to monitor on an ongoing basis for this type of signal, though he may study the formation after it takes place.

SCALING IN TRADES

Scaling in trades on a shorter time-frame reduces trading risk and allows the trader to enter a trend early and take advantage of the market that exists above the short-term, intraday speculators and below long-term position traders.

The shorter the time-frame, the lower the risk. The proportional risk between five- and 15-minute bars is the square root of three. This relationship holds true for those who trade based on volume rather than time. Specifically, risk is proportional to volatility, whether it is derived from the rate of change in price relative to time or relative to volume. Volatility, on the other hand, is proportional to the square root of time and volume. Therefore:

$$\text{Risk: Volatility and Volatility: } \sqrt{\text{Time}}, \text{ so: Risk: } \sqrt{\text{Time}}, \text{ also}$$

$$\text{Volatility: } \sqrt{\text{Tick Volume}}, \text{ so Risk: } \sqrt{\text{Tick Volume}}.$$

As traders use increasingly longer time-frames, they increase their risks by the square root of time ratio. For example, to reduce risk by half (or two times) and two being the square root of four, one must trade a time-frame one-quarter of the time-frame currently being traded. To reduce risk by a level of three, the time-frame must be reduced by a factor of nine.

To carry this further, if trading a daily chart and risk is to be reduced by a factor of 10, a trader would need to trade a three- or four-minute chart, i.e., 1/100th of a day. For most traders, this is highly impractical. Nevertheless, trading a reasonably shorter time-frame reduces risk accordingly. This can be accomplished by recognizing how most traders trade and recognizing opportunities as they arise.

Professional traders who trade single commodities generally trade medium-term trends, i.e., they hold to three- to 10-day trades. This is a fairly accurate representation of such risk/reward postures. Many private speculators trade tick or very short-term charts, taking a trade only on an intraday basis and never holding positions overnight. In this way, they minimize risk, which is a must if they are poorly capitalized and cannot withstand the overnight risk.

TICK-VOLUME BARS

The recently introduced tick-volume bar improves considerably on traditional time bar charting methodology. A tick, in this context, is a price change. A tick-volume bar of 20, for example, contains the price activity over 20 price changes, or ticks. Tick-volume and time have a similar relationship to price, making the substitution of a volume-based bar for a time-based bar straightforward.

Tick-volume bars are generated more slowly during quiet trading periods and more quickly during active periods; an active day will have more bars than a quiet day. Using tick-volume bars for the monitor and screening charts requires a bit more work than using traditional bars because the number of bars to equate to (e.g., 1/5 of a day), is not obvious, but the additional reduction in risk and improvement in accuracy is worth the effort.

To set bar length, the average number of ticks in a day is calculated and divided by three, five, and eight to see which resulting number of ticks comes close to a reasonable Fibonacci number (13, 21, 34, 55, etc.).

Many funds and portfolio traders, as well as investors who practice other professions during the trading day, trade on daily bars, only taking signals based on daily activity. Funds traders trade portfolios in order to minimize risk and are comfortable with daily bars. Many use automated trading models, which run overnight. Investors are not in a position to trade during the day and often are willing to hold small positions and suffer wide variations in equity.

Thus, traders who are free to trade during the day and are not forced to trade a portfolio or other basket of commodities can take advantage of mid-range opportunities that lie between scalpers on the floor and longer-term portfolio traders.

SETTING UP CHARTS

A trading opportunity exists in the middle range time-frames, an opportunity in a time-frame longer than that used by scalpers on the floor and shorter than that used by the daily bar and daily bar portfolio traders. This method uses a 1/5- to 1/8-day chart (about an hour) to monitor a 10- to 20-minute chart timing (1/3 to 1/5 of the monitor chart time-frame). For traders who wish to hold longer-term positions, those positions would be held based on daily bars.

To monitor and screen trades effectively, traders should use three charts: a longer-term chart to get a basic picture of what the market is doing, a shorter time-frame monitor chart in the time-frame in which they actually trade, and an even shorter time-frame timing chart to improve exits and entries. The monitor chart bars should be equal to 1/5 to 1/8 the length of longer time-frame bars; the timing chart bars should be 1/3 to 1/5 the length of monitor chart bars.

Once these charts are established, the average true range (See Sidebar, Determining True Range) of the bars in the timing chart should be large enough to be meaningful, meaning that traders must be careful that the resulting time-frame is not too small. The absolute minimum allowable average range for the timing chart is three times the tick volatility; tick volatility is defined as the average difference in price between ticks (allowing one tick to get in, one to get out, and one for commissions). For example, if the tick volatility is 0.5 cents, then three times the tick volatility is 1.5 cents. If the average true range of the timing chart bars of the market being traded is less than 1.5 cents in this case, the market is not volatile or liquid enough to trade and traders should stand aside or day-trade tick charts. (See Sidebar, Tick-Volume Bars.)

SCALING UP IN TIME EXAMPLES

Scaling up in time is illustrated by the following two examples. This first illustrates a loss and the second a win. In both cases, the results are improved using my scaling-up methodology, which are based on the results from scaling up in time-frame versus simply trading on a daily chart. For this example, the position is exited on one close against the trade below or above the slow moving average and two closes above or below the fast moving average in the longest time being traded. Thus, if a trade is taken on the timing chart time-frame and two closes have occurred against the trade above or below the fast moving average or one close has occurred above or below the slow moving average, the trader should exit *before* getting a signal from the monitor chart.

Figure 4–10 again illustrates the DMark chart, this time displayed along with shorter time-frame DMark charts that overlap; specifically included are an 80-minute chart (1/5 of a day) and a 20-minute chart (1/4 of the 80-minute time-frame).

For Figure 4–11, it is assumed that trades are entered with 50 percent of the position on a combination of a permission screen and a crossover on the timing chart. The second 50 percent, if the trader is not stopped out first, is entered on a combination of a permis-

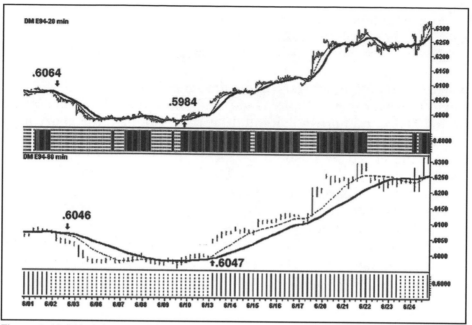

Figure 4–10 DMark Intraday Charts, 80- and 20-minute

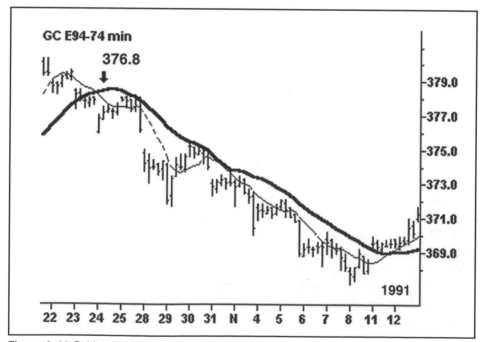

Figure 4–11 Gold 1991, Intraday Chart, 74-minute

sion screen and crossover on the monitor chart. A moving average crossover permissioned on the daily chart (see Figure 4–9) signals that it is okay to transfer contracts for tracking on the daily.

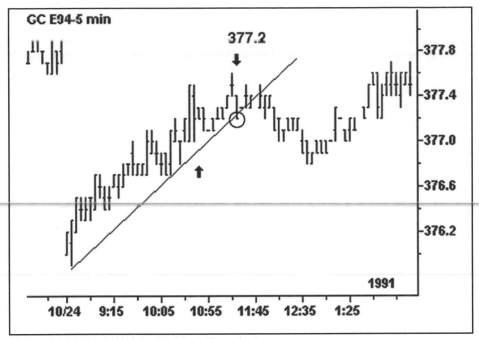

Figure 4–12 1991 Gold, Intraday Chart, Five-minute

Trade One Example:
Loss Minimized by Scaling Techniques

Looking at the crossovers toward the left of the chart in Figure 4–10 for June 2, half the trade short, say 50 out of 100 contracts, should be entered at roughly 0.6064 on the timing chart. This is followed by a permissioned crossover on the monitor chart (the 80-minute chart) at 0.6046. Thus, the trader is short 100 contracts at an average price of 0.6055.

Looking back at the daily chart in Figure 4–9, it can be noted that these signals are followed by a permissioned crossover at 0.5986 on the daily chart. The trader is then whipsawed and stopped out at 0.6068 for a 13-point loss, again, as noted on the daily chart.

If the loss that would have incurred had the trade been made on the daily chart is considered, an 82-point loss would have occurred. Again, looking back at this chart, the trader would have entered at 0.5986 and exited at 0.6068, thus the loss was reduced by almost 85 percent using the Kase Permission Screen method.

Trade Two Example:
Gain Maximized by Scaling Technique

Looking at a long trade in isolation from the earlier short trade, there is a permissioned buy on June 10 at 0.5984 on the timing chart that is followed by a permissioned buy signal at 0.6047 on the moni-

DETERMINING TRUE RANGE

True range is a measure of the maximum amount of money that can be made or lost from one bar's close to the next. This value is used in many technical analysis calculations. At face value, one might think the difference between the high and low of a bar would be an accurate reflection of this amount; but, because the market can gap up or down from the previous day's close, this gap must be considered in the calculations.

The true range is then equivalent to the maximum of the high of the most recent bar (bar [0]) minus the low of the most recent bar, the absolute value of the high of the most recent bar minus the close of the previous bar (bar [1]), and the absolute value of the close of the previous bar minus the low of the most recent bar.

True Range = maximum of:

- $High_{[0]} - low_{[0]}$, i.e., high minus low of this bar (Figure 4–13A)

- Absolute ($high_{[0]} - close_{[1]}$): the high of this bar minus previous close (Figure 4–13B)

- Absolute ($close_{[1]} - low_{[0]}$): the previous close minus low of this bar (Figure 4–13C)

The average true range is the simple arithmetic average of true range over a specified number of bars.

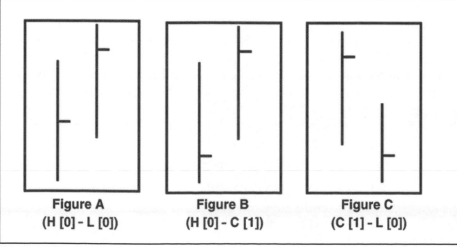

Figure A
(H [0] - L [0])

Figure B
(H [0] - C [1])

Figure C
(C [1] - L [0])

Figure 4–13

tor chart. The average of these two prices is 0.6016. The daily chart in Figure 4–9 indicates a permissioned buy at 0.6208. This trade lasts for quite a long time until there are two closes below the fast moving average. The exit price is 0.6383. This trade generated better than 367 points profit versus the 175 points that would have resulted if the trader had not scaled in and this is better than twice the profit.

Scaling-in increases the probability of success. The more of a buffer a trader has against losses, the greater the probability of his overall performance being profitable.

FINE-TUNING ENTRIES

Another technique involving multiple time-frames is an execution rather than a trading technique. The distinction here is that the decision to take a trade has already been made but is dropped down to a shorter time-frame to improve timing of the trade and save money on that execution. Figure 4–11 is a 74-minute chart (1/5 of a day) of 1991 gold. A moving average crossover at $376.80 occurred on October 24.

If we drop down to a five-minute chart, the up-arrow shows approximately the time at which the sell signal on the monitor chart is generated. Any simplistic method for timing into the market after this point is acceptable. In this case, a trend line is drawn below the bars. If the market closes below the trend line, the market can be entered. In this case, the first close below the trend line is at 377.2. The $40 per contract savings generated by using this method more than compensates for long-term commissions, which are usually in the $15- to $25-range for corporate clients.

Experience has shown that, generally speaking, this is the order of magnitude of savings that can be expected by perfecting one's market entry using the dropping down in time-frame method.

EMPIRICAL EVIDENCE THAT PRICE AND VOLUME ARE PROPORTIONAL TO THE SQUARE ROOT OF TIME

For the empirical test, we chose a data stream at random. In this case, we will look at DMark data from September 30, 1992. We first look at time, examining an eight-minute bar and multiple of that bar. If the eight-minute bar is one time unit, then a 16-minute bar is two time units, a 24-minute bar is three time units, and so on. The true range of each of these bar lengths is compared with the true range of the original eight-minute bar (see Table 4-1).

Next, the same comparison for tick volume bars is made, beginning with the 10-tick bar and going up to a 50-tick bar in increments of 10 for tick-volume units of 2, 3, 4, and 5. Again, the true range of each of our bars of the various lengths and the ratios thereof is used (see Table 4-2).

Table 4-3 indicates the square root of the time and tick-volume units next to the actual measured ratios of the true range, found by using the eight-minute and the 10-tick bars in Tables 4-1 and 4-2. It is to be noted that the ratios of the true ranges are close to the square root of the time and volume ratios. For example, in row 2, where a ratio of two occurs between the eight- and the 16-minute bar and the 10- and 20-tick bars, the square root of two is 1.41, the

Time Units	Bar Length. Minutes	Bar True Range	Ratio to Eight-Minute Bar
1	8	.0012	.0012/.0012 = 1
2	16	.0017	.0017/.0012 = 1.4
3	24	.0022	.0022/.0012 = 1.8
4	32	.0026	.0026/.0012 = 2.2
5	40	.0031	.0031/.0012 = 2.6

Table 4-1

Tick-Volume Units	Bar Tick Volume	Bar True Range	Ratio to 10 tick bar
1	10	.0005	.0005/.0005 = 1
2	20	.0007	.0007/.0005 = 1.4
3	30	.0009	.0009/.0005 = 1.8
4	40	.0010	.0010/.0005 = 2.0
5	50	.0011	.0011/.0005 = 2.2

Table 4-2

Units	Square Root	Ratio Eight-Min.	Ratio 10-Tick
1	$\sqrt{1}1$ = 1	1	1
2	$\sqrt{2}2$ = 1.41	1.4	1.4
3	$\sqrt{3}3$ = 1.73	1.8	1.8
4	$\sqrt{4}4$ = 2	2.2	2.0
5	$\sqrt{5}5$ = 2.24	2.6	2.2

Table 4-3

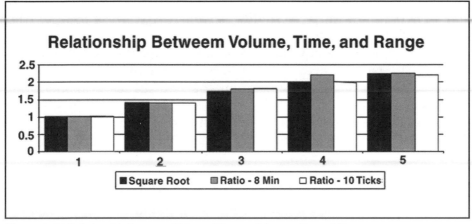

Figure 4–14 Relationship between Volume, Time and Square Root of Range

ratio of the true ranges of the eight- and 16-minute bar is 1.4, and the ratio of the 20- to 10-tick bar is 1.5.

Figure 4–14 graphically illustrates the relationships among volume, time, and true range ratios. Thus, empirical evidence supports our theoretical assertions.

The Traditional Stochastic Indicator

The Stochastic is a momentum indicator that measures the relationship of the closing price to the high/low price range over a specified number of days. The relationship is expressed as a percentage from 0 to 100. The Stochastic is based on the premise that, in a solid trend, momentum and price move in concert. Thus, in an uptrend, the closing price should be close to the high extreme for that range of days. In a downtrend, momentum moves lower with price, so that the close should tend to settle closer to the low of the high/low range. A high Stochastic value (i.e., greater than 70) indicates that the closing price is near the top of the price range for the past n bars. A low-level (i.e., less than 30) indicates that the close is towards the low end of the price range.

Thus, in a rising market, closes can be expected to be near the highs of the bars on average; and in a falling market, closes can be expected to be near the lows. When the market loses momentum, the closes fail to reach the highs or lows of the range. When closes fail to meet the appropriate extreme at either end of the range in question, it indicates that momentum is falling off, possibly signaling a change in market direction.

The Stochastic is made up of two lines that oscillate between 0 and 100, commonly called %K and %D. The most commonly used stochastic is the Slow Stochastic, which is found in many charting packages. This indicator is calculated as follows:

Step One:

Range (Rn) over n bars, calculated by

$$Rn = HH - LL,$$

where:

HH = highest high over n bars

LL = lowest low over n bars

Step Two: Initial or Fast %K, generally referred to as the Raw Stochastic, calculated by:

$$\%K = \frac{C - LL}{R_n} \times 100$$

where:

$$C = \text{most recent closing price}$$

Step Three: Fast %D, sometimes called Slow %K is calculated by smoothing (or taking an exponential moving average of) Fast %K (See Chapter 1 Sidebar, "Moving Averages"):

%D or Slow %K = [x day sum of ($C - LL$)] / x day sum of Rn)

or

$$\frac{\sum_{k=1}^{x}(CC - LL)_k}{\sum_{k=1}^{x}R_n}$$

where x is the number of days (usually three) over which to smooth the %K

Step 4: The Slow Stochastic employs the Fast %D (or Slow %K) and a Slow %D. The Slow %D is calculated by smoothing the Fast %D, once again:

%K is usually represented by a solid line;
while %D is usually represented by a dashed line.

Increasing the Probability of Catching Market Turns

Chapter Four depicted how signals can be filtered to reduce whipsaws and how multiple time-frames can help traders enter short-term or transient trends more efficiently. This is only half the battle. Advanced notice that the market may turn allows the trader to aggressively take profit on existing trades. Such warning also allows traders to improve new entries with confidence. Most traders concentrate on entry strategies and neglect exit strategies. Fine-tuning both entries and exits can greatly improve trading performance. Chapter 5 discusses improving entries and exits by identifying market turns early.

As discussed earlier, most popular technical indicators were designed prior to the advent of the personal computer. Indeed, most were designed either for calculation by hand or on a programmable calculator. Yet many traders rely solely on these low-tech indicators, even when imbedded into complex trading systems. This is akin to putting a hand-crank starter designed for a Model-T into a late-model Ford or putting a 64K RAM chip into a multi-media workstation. Relying solely on parts from outdated technology, even if those tools are used in new ways, limits results. The two new parts presented in this chapter are designed to probe the market more accurately and completely, using state-of-the-art technology. The Kase PeakOscillator and the KaseCD (KCD) are statistically based, universal indicators that catch market turns usually missed by traditional indicators.

WHY TRADITIONAL MOMENTUM INDICATORS CANNOT BE EVALUATED STATISTICALLY

The word momentum is actually borrowed from the field of physics, in which it is defined as the product of mass and velocity. In the market, we have no mass, so momentum is usually a measure of price velocity or the *rate of change* in price, i.e., how fast prices change in a given time or tick-volume period. At the simplest level, the basic formula for momentum is:

$$M = \text{close}_{\text{latest}} - \text{close}_{\text{previous}},$$

where $\text{close}_{\text{previous}}$ is the closing price of the previous bar to be measured. Because the current close may be either higher or lower than the previous close, momentum can have positive or negative values assigned to it.

Momentum in the market is actually the first derivative of price (rate of change of price) in the same way that velocity is the first derivative of distance (rate of change of distance). The point behind momentum indicators is that momentum tends to lead price.

Momentum indicators, such as the RSI, Stochastic, and MACD, evaluate the degree to which the rate of change in price is consistent with market direction. (Some momentum indicators, such as the MACD, are actually second derivative, or acceleration-related, indicators. Technicians generally lump velocity, first derivative indicators, and second derivative acceleration indicators under the general term of "momentum.")

Market momentum can be compared to the rate of change of a ball thrown in the air. As the ball nears its apex, it may still be moving higher but its rate of ascent (momentum) slows as it reaches maximum elevation. Eventually, as it reverses direction, its momentum passes through zero at the apex (from positive to negative), and then it falls back to earth. Market momentum usually degrades, just as the momentum of the ball degrades, as prices reach an apex prior to an actual reversal. This is known as momentum divergence.

Momentum divergence is the key signal generated by momentum indicators generally used to catch market turns. Prices may reach a new high, while momentum fails to do so (the ball at its peak); this is often expressed as "a higher-high in price, a lower-high in momentum," or "an unconfirmed high" and is called a "bearish divergence." Conversely, at market bottoms, "bullish divergence" is a lower-low in price not matched by a new low in momentum.

The difficulty with traditional momentum indicators is that they often fail to generate divergences and, thus, miss turns. Another reason traditional indicators may miss a turn is because there is only one high or only one low. Since divergence, by definition, requires a higher-high in price, accompanied by a lower-high in momentum or vice versa, a spike that only gives a single high or low cannot generate divergence.

WHAT IF WE COULD DEFINE OVERBOUGHT AND OVERSOLD?

The problem with traditional indicators is that they are all relative, i.e., they are all dependent on local conditions, i.e., what is happening within the recent past, and "recent past" is defined by the number of bars used in the indicator. Thus overbought and over-sold conditions are relative—depending on the recent past and having different meanings under different conditions.

The Stochastic captures the relationship between the close and the recent high-low range. It is a normalized oscillator, in that its values are forced between 0 and 100. In the Stochastic, the 0 to 100 range is determined by the high to low range over the period of the indicator. As the range changes, the values of the indicator adjust and change as well. For example, if looking at a nine-period Stochastic, local conditions would be those reflected in the last nine bars or periods (plus a couple of additional bars for smoothing).

One problem with normalized oscillators is the limits of a particular indicator change relative to external factors. Further, the limits of different commodities bear no relationship to each other at all. Thus, it is *generally* impossible to compare a Stochastic at a reading of 90 percent on crude oil in one year with the same reading in another year, unless the market is behaving in an identical fashion in both years, which is highly unlikely. Comparing crude oil in 1995 with gold in 1982 is completely out of the question.

A symptom of this problem with a normalized indicator is that the more trendy and active the market is, the less sensitive the indicator becomes. With a quiet, sideways market in which the average price swings are relatively small, minor movements in price can force the indicator to move drastically. The more trendy or active a market is, the greater the market movement required to move the indicator. The RSI is similarly limited by normalization. It measures the average of net higher closing changes for a selected time period over the average of net lower closing changes for the same period. Thus, the RSI reading is dependent on the rate of change (difference in closes) and the range of those closes, and suffers the same dependence on local conditions as the Stochastic.

Simple oscillators have the same problem. Most oscillators simply measure the differences between moving averages, such as the difference between a five- and 21-period moving average. In such a case, the oscillator itself is dependent on two variables: the time-frame and the units of the commodity. The time-frame makes a difference because the rate of change of an oscillator, the difference between two moving averages, is dependent on the time-frame one is trading. A five-period moving average on a daily chart will show a far greater rate of change than a five-period moving average on an hourly chart. The units make a difference because an oscillator tracking gold, for example, measured in dollars per ounce, will give an entirely different result than one tracking crude oil, measured in dollars per barrel.

System developers using these old techniques must test trading systems and indicator methods empirically rather than statistically by design. In other words, the indicators must be embedded in trading rules and then tested for performance experimentally. They cannot be evaluated on a stand-alone basis statistically.

If the terms overbought and oversold had true statistical or universal significance, we would have an additional "new part." Identifying conditions when momentum exceeds the higher of either the 98th percentile of the local data or the 90th percentile of historical data would provide traders with a fairly accurate true overbought or oversold condition based on historical data. At least it would be as accurate as we can realistically get. As we have shown, the problem is that traditional momentum indicators are either unit sensitive (sensitive to the time-frame in which they have been tested) or normalized (forced between 0 and 100 percent) and are, therefore, highly sensitive to local conditions, the commodity units traded, and the time-frame traded.

THE SOLUTION: THE STATISTICALLY BASED KASE PEAKOSCILLATOR

The solution is to design and use universal, statistical measures that have meaning across all time-frames and all commodities, even if measured in different units, measures that are not normalized. Normalized, conditional measures used in traditional momentum indicators depend on local background factors. Universal measures are those which can be compared across time-frames and commodities. Thus, a universally meaningful indicator can be tested statistically on a stand-alone or independent basis.

Instead of using moving averages, one can determine mathematically whether a price series is serially dependent or independent. So our problem is solved by substituting a statistical measure of trend or serial dependency (in which each value in a series is either caused or affected by the preceding value), for the moving averages normally used in traditional oscillators. I call the resulting new indicator the Kase PeakOscillator. The mathematics is derived from a subset of probability theory called *stochastic processes*, which is separate and apart from the Stochastic indicator. Statisticians use the term stochastic to describe random models. (For the mathematical calculations behind this indicator, see below, "Stochastic Processes, Monte Carlo Simulations, and Random Walk Mathematics.")

By substituting a statistical measure of trend for empirical measures, the indicator can be evaluated on a distribution curve and the 90th percentile can be chosen to determine overbought and oversold regions without relying on local conditions. This allows identification of many market turns, which traditional indicators miss.

This innovation provides a significant, ground-breaking development in the use of momentum indicators. It is no longer necessary to test indicators by experiment. Currently, with the substitution of good math, there is an indicator that can be tested statistically on an isolated, stand-alone basis. In fact, the indicator basically tests itself in that the value of the PeakOscillator in soybeans in 1985, for example, can be compared with the value of crude oil in 1995. This allows a trader to evaluate the indicator over many years of commodity history and determine a probability distribution for the PeakOscillator. (I tested my PeakOscillator over a history of 80 years.) The level which constitutes the 90th percentile of momentum (plus or minus) over this history provides a true measure of overbought and oversold conditions for this indicator.

In addition to plotting the PeakOscillator, a PeakOut line can be displayed. The PeakOut line is drawn at the 90th percentile (determined historically) or at a default of two standard deviations above the mean local data (about the 98th percentile of the local data), whichever is greater. Thus, by definition, if momentum peaks through the PeakOut line and then pulls back, there is a 90 percent chance of either a turn or a penultimate peak preceding a divergence.

A principal value of the PeakOscillator is the ability to identify non-divergent turns that all other momentum indicators miss, using the PeakOut signal, or the point at which the histogram penetrates the PeakOut line and then pulls back. I indicate valid PeakOuts automatically with a darker line in the histogram (shown in Figure 5–1). The computer determines when PeakOuts occur.

The PeakOscillator also catches divergences often missed by other indicators because it is based on a measure of serial dependency over a look-back length that adapts automatically to the most significant cycle length. This indicator performs a more thorough analysis of the market and, therefore, generates superior results.

PEAKOSCILLATOR WORKS
WHILE OTHER INDICATORS DO NOT

Figure 5–1 illustrates a PeakOut with which I correctly identified a market turn in the July 1994 natural gas contract prior to the Memorial Day weekend. This was a turn missed by most market participants. It should be noted that the slow Stochastic was non-divergent at this point, which is why those using traditional momentum indicators missed the turn. This particular move drove the market from a low of $1.80 to a high of $2.23, a move equivalent to $4,300 per contract.

Figure 5–2 illustrates how the PeakOscillator caught a traditionally non-divergent move in Eurodollars in late 1994. As of this writing, the rally in Eurodollars is still in place. This particular

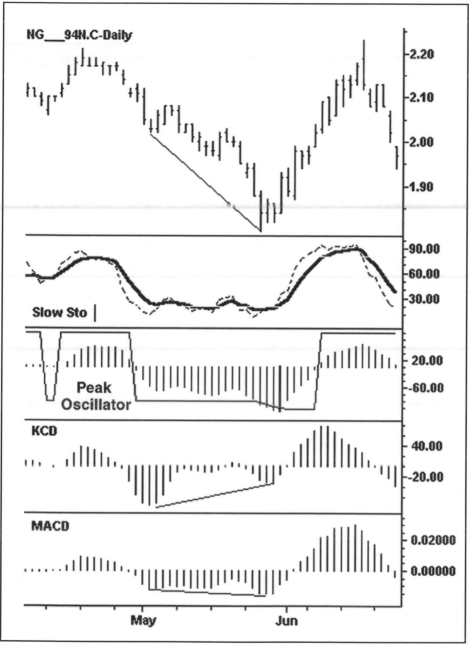

Figure 5–1 Natural Gas, July 1994

chart shows only the non-divergent RSI. The nine-period Stochastic and MACD did not show divergence either.

Figure 5–3, an intraday chart for August 1995 bean oil, illustrates the fact that the PeakOscillator may be used across time-frames (though it is helpful to remember that the market can be more trendy in shorter time-frames). The chart shows a normal default of "2" for the standard deviations of the PeakOscillator over

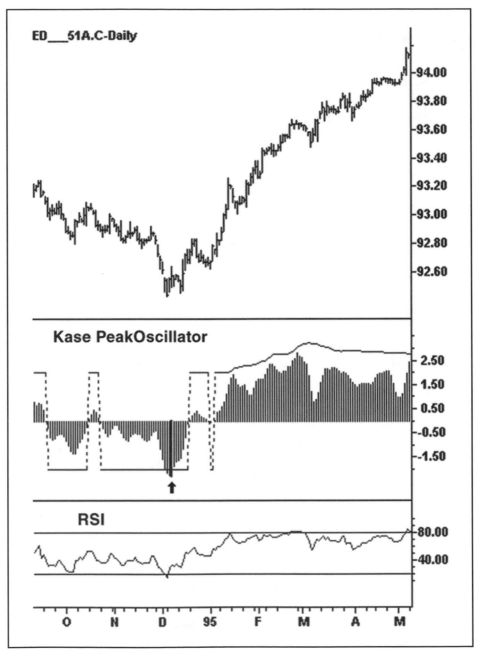

Figure 5–2 Eurodollar Continuation Chart

its local mean. (Sometimes, especially in very short time-frames, e.g. five minutes, I advise traders to increase this level to 2.5 or 3.) This chart shows a 1/5 of a day monitor chart with a clean PeakOut and a non-divergent slow Stochastic. The other traditional momentum indicators, while not shown, are also non-divergent. This PeakOut

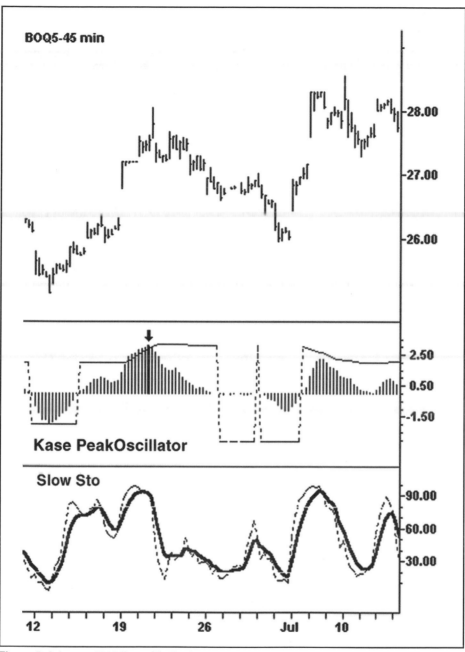

Figure 5–3 August 1995 Bean Oil 45 min.

foreshadowed the subsequent rise that resulted in a market move of $1,242 per contract.

Figure 5–4 is a 15-minute S&P chart. Of course, the 98th percentile can be modified to be less extreme for choppier markets, such as the 15-minute S&P. In this chart, I have used my customized Kase

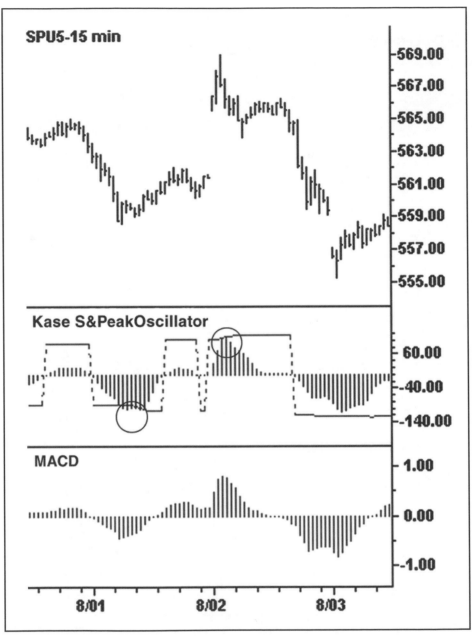

Figure 5–4 September 1995 S&P, 15-minute

S&PeakOscillator, specifically designed to catch PeakOuts on the choppy short-term S&P chart.

Figure 5–4 notes two moves (non-divergent with the MACD) catching a move up from 558.6 to 569 and back down to 555.3. This equates to a move up, worth $5,200, and a move down, worth $6,850.

IMPROVING DIVERGENCE SIGNALS
WITH THE KASECD (KCD)

Since substituting statistical measures of trend for traditional moving averages improves performance, it stands to reason that substituting statistical measures of trend for moving averages in the MACD should also attain superior results. The MACD is simply an exponential moving average oscillator minus its own average. The KCD is the PeakOscillator minus its own average.

$$\text{MACD histogram} = \text{MAO}_e - \text{average} (\text{MAO}_e, n)$$

where MAO_e is an exponential moving average oscillator (usually the difference between a 12-period exponential moving average and a 26-period one) and n = the average of MAO_e, (usually defaulted to 9).

A statistical measure of trend for moving averages can be substituted to give:

KCD histogram = PeakOscillator – average (PeakOscillator, n).

This provides superior results because the indices on which the indicator is based automatically search for the most significant cycle length and adjust to this cycle to provide a more in-depth evaluation of market behavior. This indicator is not only statistically sound but also adaptive in the sense that it elects the most significant cycle length among a variety of look-back lengths for its trend parameter.

Figure 5–5 illustrates recent natural gas continuation data and compares the KCD with the MACD. Generally, this is the same time-frame used to screen trades. In early 1995 the market turned to the upside, a turn that was entirely missed by the MACD yet was caught by the KCD.

Figure 5–6 is the same 74-minute gold chart used in evaluating the technique of dropping down in time to improve entries provided in Chapter 4. Both the peak at 380.9 and the low at 371.9 prior to the short-term corrective move up were caught by the KCD but missed by the MACD.

USING THE PEAKOSCILLATOR IN TRADING

A market turn is indicated by PeakOuts or PeakOuts followed by divergence, confirmed by either a KCD crossover or a KCD divergence. When such an indication or signal is generated, the trader should drop down to a shorter time-frame. In this shorter time-frame, PeakOuts followed by divergence will also frequently occur. Fifty percent of the trade's profit should be taken at this point and the remainder of the position exited on either tight stops (See Chapter 6) or reversals.

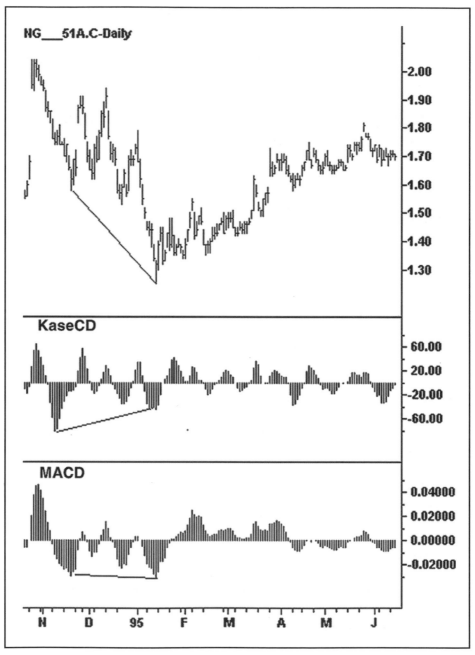

Figure 5–5 Natural Gas Continuation

In general, the longer the time-frame, the more important the signal. Important signals of change in market direction in the screening time-frame (in this case, daily) should be noted; then the trader should drop down into the monitor time-frame (1/5 to 1/8 of a day) to look for permission to take the timing signal in the opposite direction.

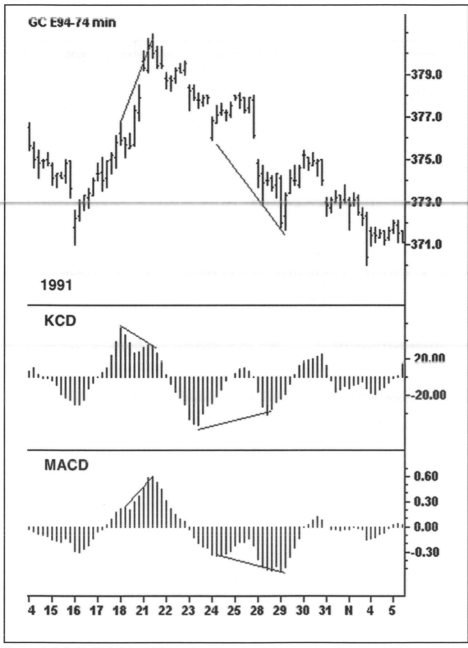

Figure 5–6 Gold, 10/21/91 74-Minute

A timing signal followed by a strong indication that the market may turn allows the trader to take that signal with more conviction and aggression. (Stops are discussed in Chapter 6. For the purposes of the following example, no stops have been used.)

Figure 5–7, the July, 1994 natural gas chart, is an example of how the PeakOscillator caught a turn that most market participants missed. The KCD confirmed this turn, while the MACD missed it.

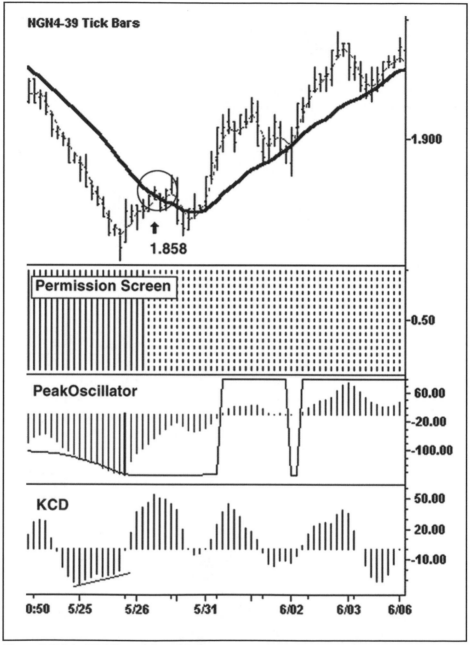

Figure 5–7 July 1994 Natural Gas, 1/8 day

A *divergence set-up* occurs when there is a lower-low in price and an unconfirmed higher-low in momentum (or vice versa). In order to be a low, the indicator value considered the low must be surrounded by higher values and vice versa. Thus, an unconfirmed low is a low, that, if followed by a higher value, will then be confirmed. A *PeakOut set-up* is the first push of the daily histogram above or below the PeakOut line, which is not confirmed by an immediate pull back in the histogram similar to the divergence confirmation above. When either set-up appears, the trader should drop down to the monitor term chart (Figure 5–7).

In this example, the chart is a 39-minute (1/8 of a day) natural gas monitor chart that indicates a PeakOut taking place on May 25th and the accompanying momentum divergence on the KCD. At this point, toward the close on the 25th, a trader can take 50 percent of the profit. Using the methodology described above, the market turn is identified by locating a PeakOut, with divergence confirmed by the KaseCD and a moving average crossover. When the permission screen changes from solid to dashed lines (see Chapter 4), the trader has permission to go long. This occurred at midday on the 26th, for an entry of approximately $1.858/mmBtu.

The trader should look closely at the moving average crossover and notice the pull back that followed. Using the methodology of dropping down further in time to improve the entry, he can position himself long at a slightly better level the following day cleanly exiting his short trade only hours after making a market low and entering a new trade on a reversal to the upside.

STOCHASTIC PROCESSES, MONTE CARLO SIMULATIONS, AND RANDOM WALK MATHEMATICS

Stochastic Processes

The study of stochastic processes is a subset of the study of probability theory. To those of us who are not statisticians, stochastic process problems are both interesting brain teasers and a sure way to a quick headache.

Statisticians generally define stochastic processes as any collection of variables defined on a common probability space, thought of as a time parameter set. A common probability space is like a mini-universe that can capture all the possible situations that might happen given a certain set of circumstances. In most stochastic processes, the past events do not influence the conditional probabilities of future events. Processes influenced by history are called Markov processes and are classified by the degree to which the past affects the present.

Stochastic processes in general involve the study of random motion. Truly pure random motion is motion in which all variables are independent, random, and normally distributed. In market terms, prices would always revert to the mean in markets exhibiting perfectly random behavior, hence the term, mean-reverting market.

It is interesting to note that first nearby contracts often do not appear to be mean reverting; but in many markets, such as energy, if all the contracts traded every day are averaged, the resultant average price, called the forward strip price, is both mean-reverting and more or less normally distributed over the medium-term (a four- or five-year period).

Studies of random motion, recently popularized in trading applications by Mike Poulous and Alex Saitta (see References) have introduced the Random Walk Index (RWI). The RWI formula is:

RWI = actual price movement/expected random walk

$$\mathrm{RW}_{high} = \frac{high_o - low_n}{ATR \times \sqrt{n}} \qquad \mathrm{RW}_{low} = \frac{high_n - low_0}{ATR \times \sqrt{n}}$$

where ATR = average true range and n = number of bars in the look back period.

RWI and the study of random motion have traditionally been used for trend measurement. In most common stochastic processes, the simplest form of the RWI is the coin toss. To illustrate this, a chart can be drawn on which each market close is either the same as or plus or minus one, relative to the previous coin toss. Over n coin tosses, the price would be expected to stay within two standard deviations of the mean, which is proportional to the square root of n. This is why price change is proportional to the square root of units shown on the x-axis of a normal bar chart. In two-dimensional space, there is a 100 percent certainty that purely random motion will revert to the mean. It is generally assumed that random prices will stay within two standard deviations of the mean.

Monte Carlo Simulations

A Monte Carlo simulation is simply a probability test in which the coin is tossed so many times that actual empirical results may be achieved. For example, a coin, when tossed, has a 50/50 probability of coming up heads or tails; pays $1.00 on heads or tails. After 100 tosses, the probability of losing $5.00 is evaluated. A computer might be programmed to toss the coin 100 times in 1,000 tests and plot the results.

Figure 5–8 notes the results of a Monte Carlo simulation as applied to the market, showing a price distribution curve for a theoretical gold contract that has a starting price of $300. We can assume that the price moves with no bias direction, i.e., with an average change of zero percent, but that it exhibits a standard deviation of 0.18 percent. After 1,000 samples over 65 days of activity, a mean expectation of $300 and a standard deviation of about $35 indicates a 95 percent confidence level that prices will be between $230 and $370.

Next we run a second experiment and note the prices after 1,000 Monte Carlo simulations over 65 days of activity, this time with an

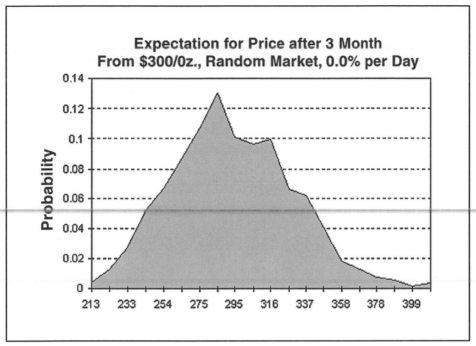

Figure 5–8 Random Market Simulation

assumed upside average bias of 1/3 percent per day and the same degree of volatility. The average or mean expectation in this case is $372, which is outside of the random simulation range. This is a case in which price fluctuations are not perfectly random, since $372 falls outside the 95 percent confidence level.

THE KASE TWIST ON THE RWI

The RWI can be used as a measure of the degree to which current market activity varies from the purely random case expressed by the first Monte Carlo simulation example. It measures the extent of the data exhibit's drift away from the mean expectation.

From a mathematical standpoint, a problem in the form of the average true range term in the RWI formula exists. (See Chapter 4 Sidebar: Determining True Range.) Since the average true range is highly erratic and unstable over small ranges, the RWI is also erratic and unstable over small ranges.

Statisticians generally use a minimum of 30 points to form a statistically significant sample. We can compare the standard deviation of the average true range, multiplied by the square root of 10 (to reflect the denominator value accurately for a 10-period RWI) over an average of 10 to an average of 30 periods to see if stability is improved.

The ratio of the standard deviation of the average true range relative to the average for both of these calculations is shown in the following table. The RWI is calculated over 10 periods in Column 2, but in Column 3 uses a 30-period average true range. Column 4 uses a triple-smoothed 30-period average true range. Four different markets are evaluated in this table on a random basis: soybean daily, May, 1994; S&P 500 Daily, March, 1993; T-bond daily, September, 1995; and crude oil, 13-minute, August, 1995.

	2	3	4	5	6
	RWI 10	RWI 10 with 30 ATR	Previous Smoothed	3, Stability vs. RWI 10	4, Stability vs. RWI 10
S94K	0.207	0.087	0.086	57.82 percent	58.36 percent
SP93H	0.262	0.191	0.189	26.90 percent	27.98 percent
US95U	0.314	0.249	0.240	20.61 percent	23.38 percent
CL95Q(13)	0.258	0.168	0.168	34.69 percent	34.77 percent

Columns 5 and 6 indicate the percentage improvement in stability generated by this mathematical change. This empirical test demonstrates an average 35 percent improvement in the stability of the RWI with the 30-period average true range and an additional one percent improvement (i.e., 36 percent) with the triple-smoothed version.

Thus, a minimum of 30 periods is employed when evaluating the range since the triple-smoothing uses computer power for little improvement.

The RWI, with our correction, forms the basis for the mathematics used in calculating the Kase PeakOscillator.

CHAPTER 6

Using Statistics to Find Optimal Stop: Kase's Adaptive Dev-Stop

The trader should now be able to improve entries by scaling up in time. He has learned to identify market turns, to take new trades more effectively, and to finesse market timing.

It is time for more pieces of the puzzle: fine-tuning and optimizing exits. This requires that traders maintain an objective perspective when following the market. The market, just like the ocean, behaves as it will according to forces over which we have no control. Successful traders learn to accept the market as it is, rather than expend effort trying to make the market conform to their own preconceived ideas and desires. The market will not go up just a little bit more because a mortgage payment is due, and it will not stop falling just because we run out of money. Successful traders learn to accept the notion "That that is, *is*," as Shakespeare wrote in *Twelfth Night* (IV, ii, 14).

One of the things I like about trading technically, as opposed to trading based on fundamental analysis or on psychological factors, is that I can study and learn about technical analyses in the same way I studied engineering. This is not true of fundamental or psychological trading (i.e., relying on intuition and such subtle behavioral clues as vocal intonation during telephone conversations with counterparties in other markets).

In my studies of technical analysis, I found a serious void in the examination of exit strategies. It was like learning to drive a car without being told where the brake pedal was! There are two reasons for this void in the literature: greed and fear. Ending a profitable trade or cutting a loss is not the fun part of trading. People don't like to lose, and many folks don't know when to call it quits. Fear of losing too much becomes a self-fulfilling prophecy when a trader hangs on too long, thinking the market will turn around. Because he cannot weather the loss, he waits and prays that the market will move in *his* desired direction.

Greed can cause winning traders to hold onto a position too long as well, as they try to milk the last drop out of a trade that is already exhausted. I often say that trading is like getting involved in a relationship: it is a lot easier to get in than to get out. Indeed, traders who have trouble with exits are said to be "married" to their position.

Another possible factor for the lack of exit information is that most of the early work in technical analysis was done on equity markets and equity market indices. No firm likes to have its stock downgraded from a buy to a hold, and, certainly, downgrading a stock from a hold to a sell is an extremely serious move. At even the whisper of such a downgrade, companies invest considerable resources in public relations to persuade sentiment in the opposite direction. Unlike the commodities market, only a few people (such as options traders) make money from shorting equities and falling prices.

THE OLD MOUSETRAP: STOPS BASED ON FEAR

Most traders set stops based on what they can afford to lose. For example, if the trader can afford to lose $5,000, he might trade 10 contracts and risk $500 per contract. This is fine if the typical fluctuations in the market and in the time-frame he is trading are less than $500, but what if they are not?

A trader who sets stops with such assumptions is like a sailor with a small boat who stands by the sea and commands that the waves be no higher than two feet because that is all his boat can handle. When he sets sail into four-foot seas, he is instantly capsized. Like the sea, the market doesn't care how big a boat is. If the waves in the sea or the risk level in the market is too great to withstand an average trading day without getting stopped out, the trader does not belong in that market. On the other hand, when trading in such a market, a trader should not set stops that will force him out on noise, regardless of whether the trade might have been profitable.

WHAT RISK DOES THE MARKET IMPOSE?

The important question, then, is not how much a trader can afford to risk, but how high are the waves. What is the market risk imposed on the trader?

Risk is directly proportional to volatility. The amount the price can change in a given interval is the amount the price can go against the trade during that interval. Volatility is the standard deviation of rate of change on an annualized basis. It is usually thought of by option traders and risk managers as the price change associated with a one standard deviation change in price anticipated over the course of a year.

One standard deviation of price change encompasses approximately 67 percent of the observations. A price that goes against a trade by one standard deviation is a move in the opposite direction of the trade encompassing 33.3 percent of the observations. For example, if volatility is 20 percent, then 67 percent of all the observations expected over the next year will fall between plus or minus 20 percent of today's price. If there is a 95 percent confidence level (or about two standard deviations), then 95 percent of the prices will be within 40 percent of today's price over the next year.

While this definition of volatility is useful when looking at long-term risks, it is not particularly helpful to traders who are holding a trade for a day or perhaps a few weeks. For these traders, I suggest using true range as a proxy for volatility. (See Chapter 4 Sidebar, "Determining True Range.") One might argue that, over the long run, prices expand or contract exponentially (or according to the logarithmic spiral); but for all practical purposes, for short to medium-term trades, the straight line expressed by the true range is a close enough approximation. Indeed, the true range relates to both time and volume in exactly the same way that volatility does.

In order to take a trade, a trader needs, at least, to be able to withstand the normal range of the bar that he is trading. This is another good reason to use the true range. For example, a trader who is employed full-time in another pursuit during normal business hours may review the market each evening. His normal methodology is to perform analyses overnight and call his broker in the morning before the market is open to place an order. He wishes to take a position in Japanese yen and decides to buy at the open, intending to hold his position for a week or two. He places a $0.50 stop on his position. Unfortunately, the average daily range in yen is actually about $0.90. He has put in a stop that is only a fraction of the daily range. The odds are that he will be stopped out in the first several days of the trade.

Realistically, a trader must evaluate the market more carefully, determining the true range for the time-frame he wishes to trade, and placing stops as a function of true range.

STOPS MUST RELATE TO THE MARKET'S THRESHOLD OF UNCERTAINTY

If a market trend is thought of as a straight line or perhaps a smooth arc exhibiting serially dependent behavior, then around this serially dependent, smooth behavior is "noise" or random stochastic behavior. We accommodate for this market behavior by placing stops far enough away from the trend to accommodate noise. If none occurs, i.e., if the trend is a perfectly smooth arc or line, then *any* alteration to the trend line or arc would, by definition, indicate a market turn. The magnitude of the noise means that we cannot simply exit on a tiny move away from the trend. We need a way to judge how much noise is normal and place stops on the outer fringes of this normal behavior. How accurately we judge noise or the uncertainty level and how closely we place our stops to the fringes of that uncertainty is part of the art of trading. If we set stops too large, we let our profits run but we do not cut our losses, and thereby assume unnecessary risk. If we set our stops too narrow, we are not assuming enough risk and may be consistently stopping ourselves out of good trades.

True range is proportional to volatility. It should be remembered that volatility describes the magnitude and frequency of price fluctuations and true range provides the upper and lower limits of those fluctuations. Knowing this, how do we improve our stops systems?

THE WILDER AND BOOKSTABER VOLATILITY METHOD

When I first started trading oil technically, I used a stop value based on average price swings consistent with the time-frame that I traded, usually 15- to 20-minute bars. This worked well for me until the summer of 1990 when the Persian Gulf Crisis occurred and volatility in the energy market more than doubled. I had grown comfortable taking approximately a $0.15 per barrel risk while trading 15- to 20-minute bars. During the Gulf Crisis, I had to drop down to a three-minute bar chart to maintain the $0.15 stops. This brought home to me the importance of having stops that were consistent with the volatility in the market.

I was studying Wells Wilder's *New Concepts in Technical Trading* at the time and came across his volatility system. I also had read Richard Bookstaber's *The Complete Investment Book*. Both books had stop and reverse systems based on the true range, specifically defaulting to three times the true range as a stop and reverse point.

I adopted the methodology of using a fixed factor, multiplied by the true range for my stop. This gave me a stop that automatically adapted to the changes in the average true range. As the average true range increased, so did my stop and vise versa. In this fashion, I gave my trades room to breath with the market. This breathing room is based on what the market is actually doing. It's like preparing to set sail after having accurately judged the average height of the waves and taking appropriate precautions.

However, I was not satisfied with this method, because simply choosing a fixed factor, such as one, two, or three, and multiplying the factor by the true range is inadequate because the level of noise is variable. This variability is not captured by an average, but by the standard deviation around the mean.

VARIANCE OF VOLATILITY

First, we need to account for the effects of variance or the standard deviation of volatility. We will assume that we wish to withstand most normal two-bar reversals. For the sake of the example below, normal is defined as constituting 97.5 percent of the bars. Our stops can be as the doorway that most (97.5 percent) of our two-bar reversals can pass through. Only the tallest sets of bars will be blocked.

For example, we will consider two different populations: Population One and Population Two. The average height of people in Population One is 5'7". This population is comprised of chorus line dancers and the standard deviation of the population is one inch. If we want 97.5 percent of that population to walk though our door, we must make our door a fraction of an inch higher than two standard deviations above the mean (5'7" plus two inches) or 5'9".

Population Two is comprised of preschool children and basketball players, so this population has short people and tall people. The average height of the people in this population is also 5'7", but the distribution around the average or mean obviously is considerably greater. The standard deviation for Population Two is five inches, so one standard deviation requires a door that is six feet tall and two standard deviations requires a door that is 6'5": the size required to enable 97.5 percent of this population to pass through it.

Extending our analogy to bars, we can see that, all else being equal, the more dissimilar the bars, the taller the door, or stop, needs to be. If the bars are similar in height, i.e., they have the same average true range, we do not need to leave as much margin for the variance in range (or height). The more widely distributed the range, the more risk must be taken to keep from being stopped out on a certain percentage of moves against the trade.

We may wish to have 97.5 percent of two bar reversals not stop us out in a given bar population. Assuming the average height of the bar is 10 cents and the standard deviation is one cent, our stop would be placed at 12 cents. In a second population in which the average height of the bars is also 10 cents, but the standard deviation is three cents, a two standard deviation stop that allows 97.5 percent of two bar reversals to pass though would be 16 cents. Thus, risk is not only related to the volatility or true range but also to the variance and standard deviation of this volatility.

THE SKEW OF VOLATILITY

Secondly, the distribution of range is not normal but is skewed to the right. This is because volatility is skewed to the right. Volatility is bounded by zero on the downside and infinity on the upside. Spikes or outliers that occur and can seem to reach toward infinity cannot be negative in range. These spikes often occur when the market is about to move *against* a position. Market phenomena, such as breakaway gaps, reversal gaps, and bullish and bearish engulfing lines in candlestick patterns, are all illustrative of increases in volatility that accompany changes in market direction. Taken as a group, these phenomena are what Larry Williams has called volatility expansions. They are characteristic of market turns. When these phenomena take an incautious trader unawares, the losses can be considerable. (See Chapter 6 Appendix, "Gaps.")

Stops should not try to allow for unusual amounts of noise or huge moves in the opposite direction of the trend. To do so would be to take on more risk than is necessary. We need to account in some normal degree for the level of skew in the market. Research has shown that this skew to the right does not really become apparent until the limit of one standard deviation is passed. There is, however, a need for a correction of about 10 percent on the second standard deviation and 20 percent on the third standard deviation to adjust adequately for the skew of true range.

ENGINEERING A BETTER STOP:
THE KASE DEV-STOPS

What all of this boils down to is that we need to take variance and skew into consideration when we are establishing a system for setting stops. Three steps that we can take in order to both better define and to minimize the threshold of uncertainty in setting stops are:

1. Consideration of the variance or the standard deviation of range.

2. Consideration of the skew, or more simply, the amount at which range can spike in the opposite direction of the trend.

3. Reformation of our data to be more consistent (this step is examined in detail in Chapter 8), while minimizing the degree of uncertainty as much as possible.

THE DEV-STOP IS AS CLOSE AS POSSIBLE TO THE BEST BALANCE

We cannot eliminate all uncertainty. The precise degree of skew is highly variable, so our stop can never be perfect. However, the Dev-Stop gives us the best compromise between letting profits run and cutting losses. I normally use a three-level stop (1, 2, 3 standard deviations of a two-bar reversal above the mean), with the mean used as a warning line. All of the above is corrected for skew.

The Dev-Stop, together with accelerated stops based on candlestick patterns, comprise the portfolio of stops I normally employ. From time to time, I also use inactivity and breakaway stops.

CHARTING THE DEV-STOP

As discussed, I display the Dev-Stop using four lines. The first line, called the warning line, reflects the average two-bar reversal against the trend. The second, third, and fourth lines reflect one, two, and three standard deviation moves against the trend, corrected for skew. Since the computer has no way to tell if the trader is long or short at any given time, I also program a simple double-moving average defaulted to 10- and 21-periods into the code to default the stops to either a long or short position. (I use these moving averages simply as a clue for the computer program to generate the graphic representation of the Dev-Stop. I do not recommend using simple moving averages as critical information on which to base trades!) If the 10-period moving average is above the 21, I display the Dev-Stop below the bars, trailing a long position. If the 10-period moving average is below the 21, the Dev-Stop is displayed above the bars, trailing a short position. (These moving average lengths are variables and may be changed by the trader to speed crossovers on quick reversals and to slow crossovers in nicely trending markets.)

Under normal circumstances, I concentrate on stop level three. However, during highly volatile periods or if I am in a profit-taking mode, I use stop level one. I also assume that two closes beyond the warning line is the same as breaking stop one.

USING CANDLESTICK PATTERNS TO ACCELERATE EXITS

Candlestick charts have been in use in Japan for centuries and have recently been popularized in the West. While traditional bars tend to emphasize closing price and, to a lesser degree, the high and low, candlestick charts emphasize the relationship between opening and closing prices.

Figure 6–1 illustrates typical candlesticks. In an up-session, where the close is above the open, the candlestick is not solid but

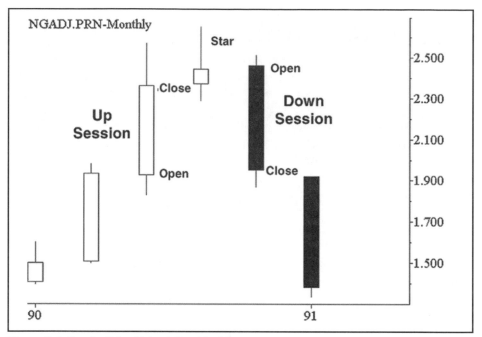

Figure 6–1 Candlesticks, Natural Gas Monthly

left blank. In a down-session, where the open is above the close, the candlestick is solid. The space between the open and close is called the body or real body, and the lines above and below are called the shadows. The shadow lines indicate the high and low of the period, just as traditional bars do.

A star is a candlestick in which the open and close are near in price. In stars, it never matters whether the star is blank or solid because the open and close are so close together that the difference is negligible.

FIVE IMPORTANT CANDLESTICK PATTERNS FOR FINESSING EXITS

There are five commonly identified candlestick patterns that are particularly helpful in identifying market turns. However, since these patterns may fall randomly on a chart, they should be used more to form confirmation than as signals in and of themselves. I look for a candlestick pattern that is coincident with evidence that the market might turn, such as a PeakOut, PeakOut with divergence, or divergence on the KaseCD.

In a bull market, a Harami Line and Star (see Figure 6–2) in the candlestick pattern is a high range up-day (blank), followed by a star that is entirely contained within the candlestick of the up-day. This is a bearish signal. In a bear market, the Harami line is a solid candlestick, also followed by a star that is totally enclosed within the candlestick body.

The set of patterns in Figure 6–3 are visually identical to each other, but they give different signals depending on what the market is doing at the time. In a bull market, this pattern is called a hanging man and is a bearish sign. In a bear market, it is called a hammer and is a bullish sign. Both the hammer and hanging man are characterized by a star body with a long lower shadow. I have found that hanging men and hammers, by themselves, tend to be leading indicators or secondary patterns on corrections. They do not tend to be coincident with major market lows or highs. However, when the star in a larger candlestick pattern contains a hanging man or hammer, the pattern itself becomes more significant.

The evening star and morning star formations in Figure 6–4 are similar to the Harami line and star in that both evening and morning stars contain a Harami line. The bearish evening star formation begins with a blank Harami line, and the bullish morning star pattern begins with a solid Harami line. Again, the line is followed by a star, but this time the body of the star is outside of the body of the Harami line. In the case of the evening star, it is above the Harami line and, in the case of the morning star, it is below the Harami line. This star is followed by a solid Harami line in the

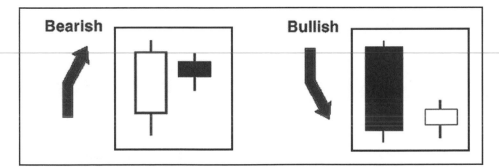

Figure 6–2 Harami Line and Star

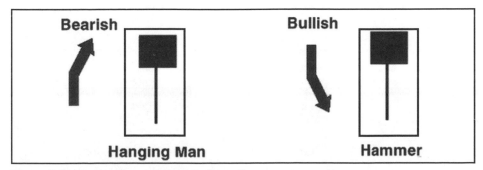

Figure 6–3 Hanging Man and Hammer Formations

evening star formation and a blank Harami line in the morning star formation.

It should be noted that the middle star pattern, in the evening and morning stars, is both proceeded and followed by a window that is parallel to a gap pattern in a traditional bar chart. These gap or window patterns are analogous to exhaustion and break-away gaps that are also reliable reversal patterns.

The bearish and bullish engulfing patterns shown in Figure 6–5 denote market turns in bull and bear markets, respectively. As the term engulfing suggests, a bearish and bullish engulfing line totally engulfs or encloses the previous candlestick. In other words, they show a higher-open and lower-close than the previous candlestick, or vice versa The only difference is that the bearish closes down and is, therefore, solid, and the bullish closes up and is, therefore blank.

Figure 6–6 illustrates the dark cloud cover and the bullish piercing pattern formations. These are, in a sense, second cousins to the bullish and bearish engulfing patterns, the only difference is that these patterns penetrate deeply into, but do not engulf, the previous candlestick. In the case of the dark cloud cover, we look for a close below the mid-point of the previous candlestick. In the case of a bullish piercing pattern, we look for a close above the mid-point of the previous candlestick.

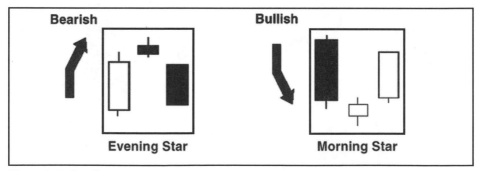

Figure 6–4 Star Formations

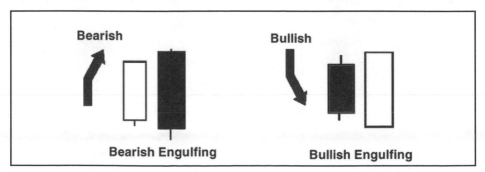

Figure 6–5 Engulfing Formations

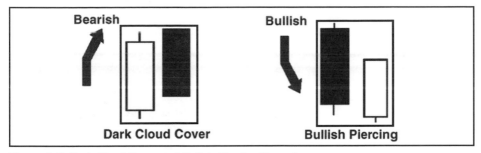

Figure 6–6 Dark Cloud Cover and Bullish Piercing Formations

ACCELERATING EXITS USING CANDLESTICK PATTERNS

With the exception of the hammer and hanging man, all the patterns may be used to accelerate exits.

The patterns that generate a warning or set-up ahead of time are the evening and morning stars. Since these are three-candlestick patterns, when two are showing, we know that all we need is a third to complete the pattern. In a two-candlestick pattern, we do not know whether the pattern is complete until the second candlestick is actually drawn.

A set-up, that is a Harami line followed by a possible exhaustion gap and star, alerts us to watch for a third candlestick to complete the pattern. We now pull our first level stop into the midpoint of the first candlestick. For example, if we are in an evening star formation and the third day in the formation is a down day, once it appears that we will close below the mid-point of the blank Harami line, we will exit the portion of the trade that we normally would exit on Dev-Stop one.

In the engulfing, dark cloud and piercing patterns, if there is a Harami line in the proper direction (blank in a bull market and solid in a bear market) that is coincident with an extreme in momentum or divergence, then we would watch for a pattern to complete itself. If there should be a higher gap in the case of a turn against a bull market or lower in the case of a turn against a bear market, we would watch for a close against the previous direction relative to the midpoint of the previous bar.

In the case of the Harami line and star, we would look for closes against the open of the Harami line. In the case of a bearish pattern at the top of the bull market, we would watch for a close of the candlestick following the star that is below the open of the blank Harami line. We would look for the opposite in a bear market. Again, we would substitute this level for the first level Dev-Stop that we would otherwise use.

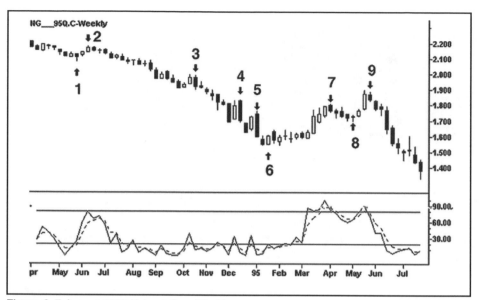

Figure 6–7 August 1995 Natural Gas, Weekly

Thus, we are becoming more aggressive in our exits, based on the candlestick patterns and using the patterns to determine exactly where the exit point would be.

An Example of Accelerated Exits Using Candlestick Patterns

Figure 6–7 charts the August, 1995 Natural Gas Contract. In this example, we use a fast Stochastic to signal extremes in momentum. It is important to note that I generally screen candlestick patterns, only paying attention to those signals that are confirmed by other indicators.

At point 1 is a hammer at the bottom of the first wave to the downside. The Stochastic low, which slightly precedes this level, is at zero. At point 2, there is a Harami line and star, coincident with a peak of the %K just slightly above the 75 percent point. This Harami line and star marks the top of a minor correction. At points 3, 4, and 5, there are bearish engulfing lines coincident with minor peaks in the %K above the 25 percent mark. These points are also coincident with tops of minor corrections. The completion of the bullish morning star formation occurs at point 6. This is not only coincident with low %K values but also with some divergence in this area.

At point 7, there is a dark cloud cover coincident with the %K at 100 percent, followed by a little hammer at point 8 at the bottom of a minor correction, which fell below the 75 percent mark. Finally, at point 9, a Harami line and star is coincident not only with a high %K value at above 90 percent but also with bearish divergence. Thus, we can see that many market turns were signaled coincident with the patterns discussed.

Stops are a critical tool for the successful trader. Traders cannot pay too much attention to the strategies for exiting markets, both to protect them from losses and to maximize their gains.

USING THE DEV-STOP IN TRADING

Figure 6–8 charts our Eurodollar data from late 1994 through the first half of 1995. The PeakOut in December, 1994 identified a sharp market turn. At point *a,* there were two closes above the warning line, the second of which followed the PeakOut.

Traders holding short positions would have exited here, just a few points above the market bottom. The up-trend on the chart shows that the third level stop held all the way through points *b* and *c,* which only touched the second level stop on reversals. At point *d,* there is a classic divergence following a PeakOut. At this point the trader would have exited 50 percent of his position and pulled in my stops either to stop level one (or two closes below the warning line). The close below the warning line occurred on the day following the peak. That close also broke the first level Dev-Stop. Thus, the trader would have exited his long position not too far down from the peak of the market, after holding the trade for about six months.

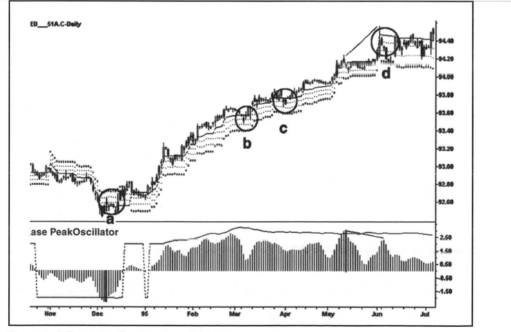

Figure 6–8 Eurodollar Continuation, 1994–95

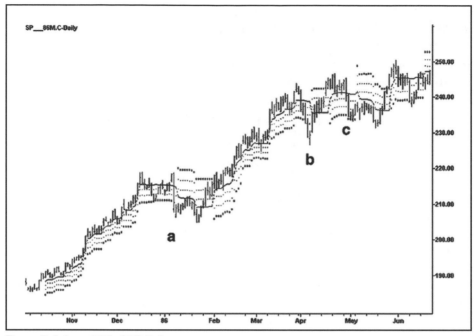

Figure 6–9 June 1986, S&P Daily

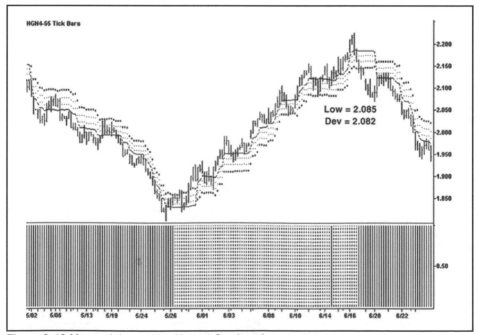

Figure 6–10 May and June 1994, Natural Gas Intraday

The S&P daily chart in June, 1986 (Figure 6–9) demonstrates that the data is much choppier than the Eurodollar contract data. In this case, all the major corrections broke the third level of the

Dev-Stop. However, there were no false breakthroughs. The Dev-Stop held all the trending periods of the move.

We note the intraday data from May and June of 1994 in Figure 6–10, which shows the turn caught by the PeakOscillator. Just after the PeakOscillator caught the turn and before the trade was permissioned to go long, there were two closes above the warning line. Following the exit and reversal, the market moved up cleanly, holding the third level stop until the peak and reversal in the opposite direction. We note from this how cleanly the Dev-Stop holds the market activity along the entire length of this chart. The profit generated by the trade caught by the PeakOscillator early in the move was preserved by using the Dev-Stop.

The October 1995 contract 30-minute S&P chart in Figure 6–11 clearly shows not only how quickly the Dev-Stop gets us out of the market on the turn at the bottom of the trend, but also how it contracts as volatility slows toward the upper part of the trend on July 26 and 27.

The Dev-Stop accurately identifies which reversals are significant and which are not. It helps determine the optimal balance point between allowing profits to run and cutting losses. The computer-generated Dev-Stop holds trending markets and assists the trader in exiting divergent or turning markets. The third level Dev-Stop holds moderate corrections. Because the moving average crossover system is used to default the Dev-Stop, long or short, we can use the Dev-Stop not only as an exit tool, but as a confirmation of entry in the opposite direction.

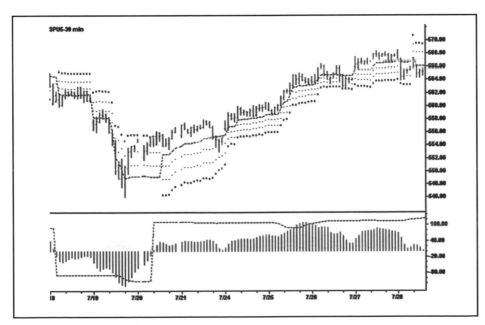

Figure 6–11 September 1995 S&P 30-Minute

Gaps

INTRODUCTION

A gap is simply an un-filled section on a price chart. Defined mathematically, a gap in an up-market occurs when the low of the current day is above the high of the previous day. The opposite occurs in falling markets. One myth is that gaps are always filled. This is not so, and, indeed, whether gaps are filled provides important information on the market. Strongly trending markets do not fill gaps in the direction of the trend. We will review four types of gaps: common, measuring, breakaway, and exhaustion gaps.

COMMON GAP

A common gap is a gap that usually occurs for no special reason other than lack of activity. Generally, common gaps should be ignored. Figure 6A–1 gives an example of a common gap.

MEASURING GAP

A measuring gap (also called mid-point or run-away gap) generally occurs midway in a trend. Thus, one can estimate the extent of the trend by adding the first leg of the trend, before the gap to the low (in an uptrend), or deducting from the high (in a downtrend) after the gap. Measuring gaps are illustrated in Figures 6A–1 through 6A–3.

BREAKAWAY GAPS

Often, new trends begin with a surge of activity and increase in volatility, which causes a gap. This type of gap is called a breakaway gap. In this case, if the gap is filled, the breakaway gap was a false signal.

Figure 6A–3 is an intraday natural gas chart. The bar size used is 34 ticks per bar, or about 1/5 of a day. The time period in question, September 1993, was characterized by a zigzag up and down market. After the market rises, a breakaway gap occurs on the reversal back to the downside.

Also noted is a gap about halfway into the move, which is the measuring gap we examined earlier. Finally, we can note an exhaustion gap just prior to the turn to the upside, toward the end of the prior down move. Prior to the exhaustion gap is a measuring gap in the move down preceding the exhaustion gap.

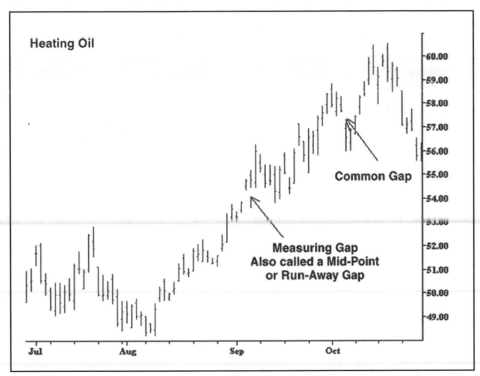

Figure 6A–1 Measuring Gap and Common Gap, 1989

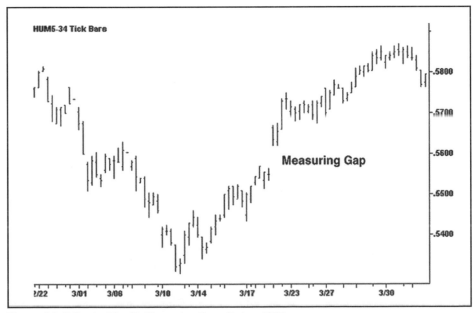

Figure 6A–2 Crude Oil with Measuring Gap, Spring 1995

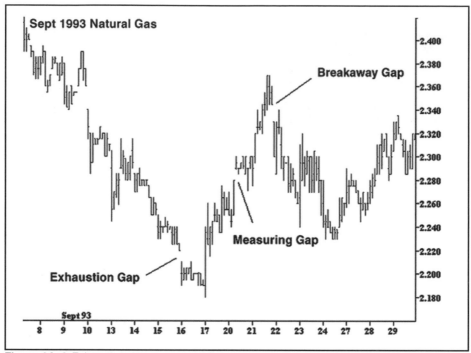

Figure 6A–3 Exhaustion, Measuring and Breakaway Gaps

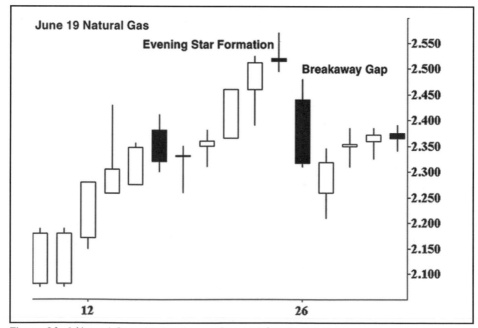

Figure 6A–4 Natural Gas with Breakaway Gap and Candlestick Pattern

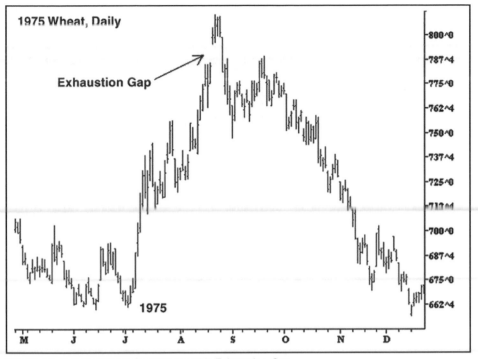

Figure 6A–5 Daily Wheat Continuous with Exhaustion Gap

EXHAUSTION GAP

An exhaustion gap occurs when trends experience a phase we call the last hurrah, which is characterized by a push in the direction of the trend caused both by latecomers jumping in speculatively after a trend has been strong enough to call for media attention and by losers who have waited until the pain has become so great that they cannot withstand it any longer and bail out.

If breakaway and measuring gaps have already been seen, a gap near the target area should occur. We can reasonably assume this to be an exhaustion gap. Even if a breakaway or measuring gap are not seen (see Figure 6A–5), if a gap is noted after a major run, we may well suspect an exhaustion gap. Filling such a gap confirms the gap. In cases in which an exhaustion gap is suspected, it is prudent to exit at least a portion of the trade if the gap is filled.

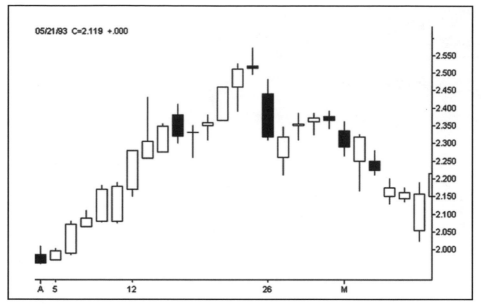

Figure 6A–6 Breakaway Gap and Evening Star Signals Reversal

CHAPTER 7

Walking through Trades

This book has described a number of new techniques designed to provide the trader with better tools for analyzing the markets than have been available to date. Any set of indicators or methods must be incorporated into a cohesive strategy and rule-based plan in order to be effective in trading the markets. This chapter pulls together all the methods discussed in earlier chapters and shows the reader how these may be used in real trading to improve profitability, while reducing risk.

In each of the following examples, two to four months of trading activity has been condensed into text and charts that may be reviewed in a few hours. The trading methodology has been simplified somewhat from "real life" trading situations, but the trader is still required to approach these trade simulations with patience. Just as a physics or calculus text cannot be approached in the same manner as recreational reading, these examples will take time and effort to work through.

There is no way to skirt around the work that is needed to compete successfully in the markets; however, we trust that a careful study of the trades in this chapter will give the reader valuable insights, not only into how to use the Kase methodology, but how to better trade with a professional approach.

TRADE PLAN FOR EXAMPLE TRADES

For the purpose of these examples, the following rules shall apply:

1. Set-up a series of multiple time frame charts (see Chapter 4), using the weekly, daily, monitor, and timing charts.

2. Watch the daily and weekly charts for signs that the market may be turning. The warning signs are:

   • The existence of a candlestick pattern (see Chapter 6).

   • A PeakOut or PeakOut followed by divergence.

   • A KaseCD divergence.

   • Set-ups of all of the above. (A PeakOut set-up occurs when the PeakOscillator or histogram pokes above the PeakOut

111

line, but is not followed by an immediate pull-back. Divergence set-ups occur when an extreme, i.e., a confirmation of a high or low, would result in a completed divergence.)

3. When warning signs appear on the weekly and/or daily charts, look for confirmation on the monitor chart.

4. If a signal is received following the signs sought in Step 3, take a confirmed signal on the timing chart on half the volume to be traded. If a signal is received that is NOT following the signs sought, wait for a second confirmed signal on the timing chart to enter the trade.

5. After placing the first half of the trade, monitor both the timing and monitor charts.

6. If a valid signal takes place on the monitor chart or a second signal takes place on the timing chart, place the second half of the trade provided the trade is still intact and has not been stopped out. The second portion of the trade will be taken, based on whichever signal takes place first.

7. Examine the trade on the daily chart. Once a signal takes place on the daily chart, the trade can be moved up to this time frame. However, before moving up, make sure that a pullback is not imminent on the monitor. If a pullback is imminent, wait to see if the market will hit stops before switching over to the daily chart.

8. On an ongoing basis, evaluate target prices, nodes, and possible turning points.

TIMING SIGNALS

Signals used (Steps 4 and 5), for the purpose of this example are:

1. Buy Trigger: Buy when the fast moving average crosses from below to above the slow moving average AND the Kase Permission Screen confirms the signal. (A 5-period simple fast moving average and a 13-period simple slow moving average are used in this example. In reality, any combination of moving averages or other simple timing method can be used.)

2. Sell Trigger: Sell when the fast moving average crosses from above to below the slow moving average AND the Kase Permission Screen confirms the signal to go short.

3. Common Sense Rule: It is always wiser to take trades just prior to the end of the day as signals are generated than

to wait until the following morning. The possibility of a gap should never be discounted.

Monitor/Timing Chart, Exit Rules and Stops

The monitor/timing chart exit rules and stops are:

1. Maintain stops at level 3 if no danger is present, but always monitor for warning signs (as defined in number 2 of the plan) when trading in direction of the trade.

2. When warning signs appear on the monitor chart, including either a PeakOut with KaseCD divergence or a PeakOut followed by PeakOscillator divergence, take half of the profit and pull the stop in to Dev-Stop one.

3. Take the second half of the profit when Dev-Stop one has been broken, remembering that two closes against the warning line or a candlestick-based stop point under these circumstances is considered equivalent to Dev-Stop one.

4. If a timing signal is received before stops are hit, stop and reverse 50 percent of the trade position.

5. If second entry timing signals are received before a stop is hit, stop and reverse on the second half of the trade.

6. If stops are hit before new signals are generated in the opposite direction, exit the trade.

Daily Chart, Exit Rules and Stops

When danger signs appear on the daily charts, traders have a number of choices, depending upon their risk postures and the amount of work they wish to do. The daily chart rules are::

1. Follow the same exit rules listed above.

2. Modify the rules by exiting on the first signals in an opposite direction and waiting for a second confirmation for entry, since many turns against the major trend (which would be traded on the daily chart) will often be corrective.

3. Take profits on stops 1, 2, and 3.

Forecasting Rules

The rules used in forecasting are those set forth in Chapter 3.

WALKING THROUGH A TRADE USING THE KASE RULES AND INDICATORS

Example One: August 1995 Natural Gas

The first example evaluated is a trade (or series of trades) that took place over the course of the spring of 1995 in the August, 1995 natural gas contract. The trade evaluation begins with an identification of a reversal pattern on a daily candlestick chart for August, 1995 natural gas (see Figure 7–1 and Chapter 6). This chart provides the first indication that the current trend may be in for a stall or reversal.

The chart shows that on May 19, there is a completed Harami line and star, coincident with *divergence* on the traditional fast Stochastic; thus, there is a significant candlestick reversal pattern, confirmed by momentum.

The $1.895 price is a *50 percent retracement* of the long downtrend from March of 1994, when the high reached $2.244, to January, 1995, when the low reached $1.545.

The calculation is $1.545 subtracted from $2.244 and divided by two; that number is subtracted from $2.244. Thus:

50% retracement = $2.244 − [0.5 × ($2.244 − $1.545)] = $1.895

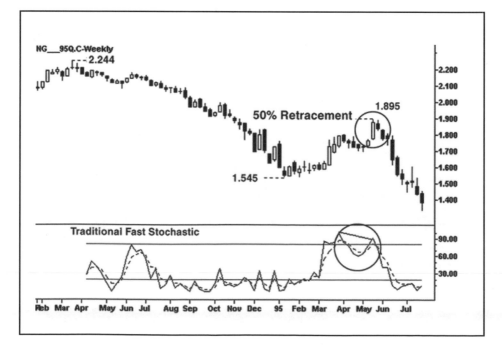

Figure 7–1 Weekly NGQ5 Chart with 50 percent Retracement

The combined signals of the confirmed candlestick reversal pattern, coincident with a major target—the 50 percent retracement—indicate a high probability that the market may turn. According to the trade plan, the daily chart (Figure 7–2) can now be evaluated for confirming signs of a possible turn.

Looking at the daily chart, we can see signs of confirmation. On May 18, the PeakOscillator poked above the PeakOut line. This sign was followed by a higher high on the histogram, which poked above the PeakOut line on the 19th. Both signs are PeakOut set-ups rather than true PeakOuts and both are bearish signals. To be an actual peak, the histogram line that pen-

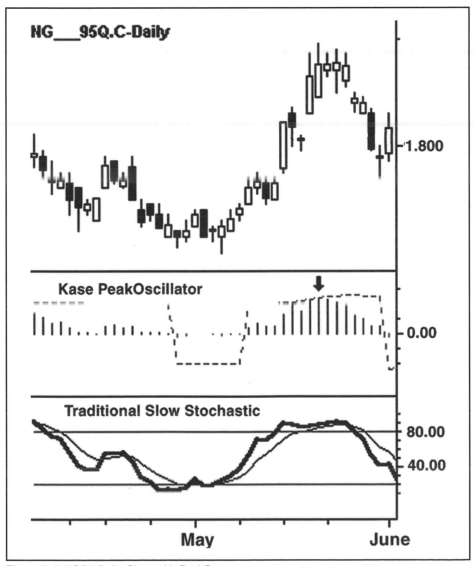

Figure 7–2 NGQ5 Daily Chart with PeakOut

etrates the PeakOut line would have to be followed by a shorter histogram line.

The PeakOut set-up, as described in the general plan, is the warning to watch for a market turn. Since the market has been in an up-trend and the Harami line and star formation are bearish signals, the trader should look for an opportunity to sell short. Although the formation on the weekly chart was not totally complete until the 19th, the divergence was already clear, and the Harami line and star were fairly well formed by the close of business on the 18th. (The traditional Stochastic indicator on the daily chart failed to generate a divergence signal at this point, again highlighting the value of the PeakOscillator.)

Again, following the general plan, the trader should look at the monitor chart next, seeking confirmation (Figure 7–3). The bars of a monitor chart are to be in the range of 1/3 to 1/5 the length of the daily bars. In this case, since natural gas trades for 310 minutes per day, a 1/5 of a day-bar is a 62-minute bar.

The monitor chart shows that, shortly after the open on the 19th, price attained a new high and the Kase PeakOscillator made a lower high. This is a confirmed divergence signal, which, in turn, confirmed the PeakOut signal that took place a few days earlier. The PeakOut, followed by divergence, was also confirmed by KaseCD divergence (shown below the Kase PeakOscillator) and is an extremely strong signal of an imminent market turn.

Per the plan, once a strong, confirmed warning occurs, the timing chart is to be analyzed for the first good opportunity to take a

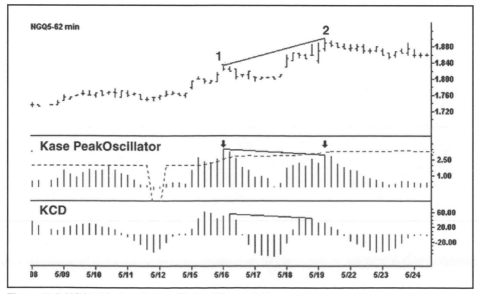

Figure 7–3 NGQ5 Monitor Chart with PeakOut and Divergence

short trade. The monitor chart in this example is a 62-minute bar chart. Since approximately 1/3 of a 62-minute bar is a 21-minute bar, the timing chart uses a 21-minute bar (Figure 7–4). The timing chart confirmed the warnings on the longer time-frame charts, with divergence on the PeakOscillator and the KaseCD. On the timing chart, the fast moving average crossed from above to below the slow moving average. The Kase Permission Screen also generated a permission short signal. These two signals in combination form a sell trigger. The arrow indicates the actual sell position, where the moving averages actually crossed, and the Permission Screen generated a permission short signal.

As we stated earlier in our common sense rule, it is always wiser to take trades just prior to the end of the day as they are generated than to wait for the following morning. While, in this case, we do not have a gap open the following morning, it is not unusual for this to happen. Thus, it is always a good idea to follow through prior to the close in order to beat the rest of the crowd.

Thus, for the purposes of our example, we will assume that we were filled on the close for 50 percent of our position, which is also the low of the bar at $1.875.

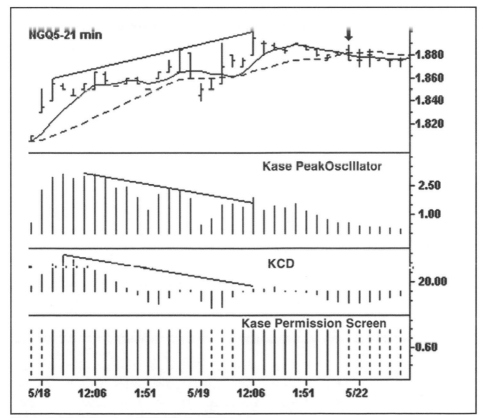

Figure 7–4 Sell Signal on NGQ5 Timing Chart

The second 50 percent of the position is to be executed either on a rally and renewed sell trigger on the timing chart or on a confirmation on the monitor chart.

In this case, we receive a confirming signal on the monitor chart, i.e., a moving average crossover to the downside, at 12:04 p.m. on Monday 23, 1995 at $1.855 confirmed by the Permission Screen generation of a permission short signal.

In this case, the trader should now drop down to a very short-term time frame, generally a tick chart, to fine-tune the entry. It should be remembered that the purpose of this strategy is to find the best point of entry rather than to look for a signal; the signal has already been generated on the monitor chart. Also, because the trader is entering the market on a pullback or minor correction, the price activity is in opposition to the overall direction of the trade. In this case, he is taking a short trade on a minor pullback to the *up*side.

The tick chart in Figure 7–5 shows that $1.855 (just two cents below our sell signal point) is a low supported all morning on the tick charts, as shown by the dotted line. At this point, there is some mini-divergence in this area. This minor divergence is indicated by the little triple bottom on the tick chart and the up-sloping Stochastic below. The lows are equal to each other, but momentum is increasing. Thus, given the divergence, there is reason to expect a minor bounce that will allow a short to be executed at a slightly better price.

This is the time to put in a sell-stop *to enter* the second half of the trade. To avoid missing the trade altogether, we will put our initial stop at a point marginally below $1.855 if we fail to bounce up. Again, we will look for a just slightly better timing point for entry. Using the single tick chart optimization technique (see Chapter 4), every time price makes a higher low, the trader is to move the sell-stop point up. The last higher low is at $1.875. At this point, the stop should be raised to $1.875. In this case, the penetration of the support level took place about 15 minutes prior to the close. Thus, the second half of the position would have been filled near the close of May 24 at $1.875, two cents better than the point at which the trade was triggered.

The full position can now be executed on the short side. The trader should follow the trade until he gets a buy signal or is stopped out.

The market traded cleanly and uneventfully downward, holding below the Dev-Stops and generating no signs of danger on the monitor chart. We received a confirmed sell signal on the daily chart, which is coincident with a threat of a minor turn to the upside, based on a morning star set-up, as shown on Figure 7–6. Thus, we will

wait to see if the market holds stops before switching over to the
daily chart.

This short trade remains fully intact throughout the first
three weeks of June as the market moves lower. Prices not only
hold well below the Dev-Stops, but do not even close above the
warning line. Indeed, our third level Dev-Stop generates a value
of $1.831, while the high of the retracement is contained at $1.83.
Thus, as we come off this minor correction, we switch over to
monitoring the trade on the daily chart.

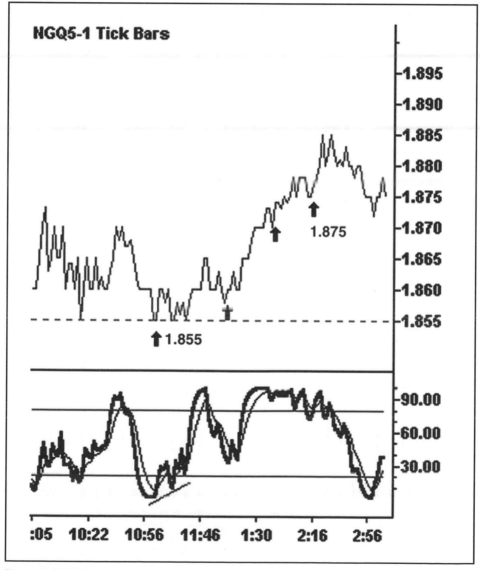

Figure 7–5 NGQ5, Improving the Entry

On June 21, the PeakOscillator touched the PeakOut line on the daily chart (see Figure 7–7). This was, once again, a warning to pay closer attention to the market and look for a confirming signal. Over the next week, the market moved lower, as did the PeakOscillator. On July 6, as traders returned from the 4th of July holiday, the market made a new low, which generated both PeakOscillator divergence and morning star formation set-ups. It should be remembered that the combination of a morning star set-up and PeakOscillator divergence is a strong warning that the market may turn.

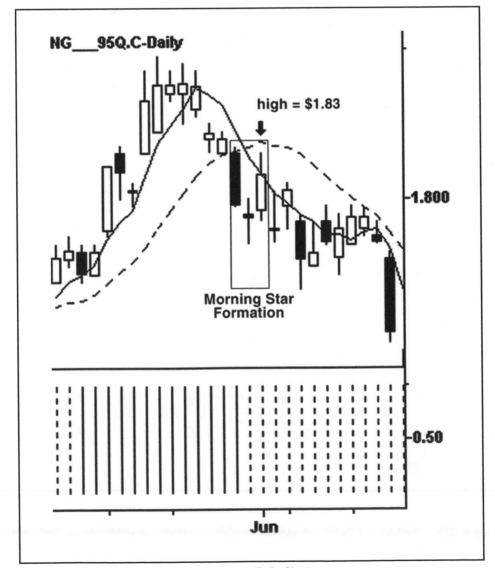

Figure 7–6 NGQ5 Sell Signal and Correction on Daily Chart

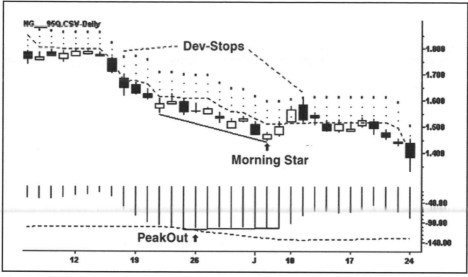

Figure 7-7 NGQ5 Daily The Market Corrects and Stops Hold

The morning star set-up is a bullish signal that indicates a possible upturn in the market. This information may be used to reposition stops according to the candlestick pattern stop rules set forth in Chapter 6. According to these rules, the halfway point of the solid Harami line should become the point at which the first level stop is positioned. The solid Harami line on July 5 opened at $1.51 and closed at $1.472, with a halfway point of $1.491.

Again, in accordance with the trading plan, half the profit should be taken if the market appears ready to close above $1.491, which would be indicated by the market trading at or near this level late enough in the day for the trader to view the probability of a close in this area as high. For this example, the arbitrary cut-off time to decide if the market will close above this level is set at 12:00 noon.

The other half of the profit should be taken if the charts, with indicators updated on a live basis, indicate that divergence will be confirmed again anytime after the arbitrary 12:00 noon cut-off line. This is consistent with exit rule 2.

Long trades are to be entered using the same, but inverse, rules as for short trades.

As stated in the rules, whenever a trade already exists, a new entry signal in the opposite direction that precedes hitting of a stop may be used both as a new entry as well as a stop on part of the existing trade. This is called a stop and reverse; the trader is exiting a trade in one direction and entering a new trade of the same size in the opposite direction. Since the trade plan for these examples calls for entering trades in halves, if an entry for 50 percent of a new position is received, a trader is also to exit 50 percent of his existing position.

According to the plan, once a trade is followed on the daily chart, the trader has some discretion as to how aggressively he will exit existing trades and enter new ones. For this example, an active trader is one who exits his trade carefully to conserve profit and takes a new trade in the opposite direction on a clear signal to get into the opposite direction as early as possible.

For an active trader approach, the charts in Figures 7–8 and 7–9 should be noted. These are the timing (21-minute) and monitor charts (62-minute), respectively.

At point 1 (in Figures 7–8 and 7–11) on the 7th, the moving averages crossed and the permission screen confirmed a signal to go long on the timing chart. This occurred at 10:21 a.m. at a price of $1.48. At this point, according to the trading plan, a

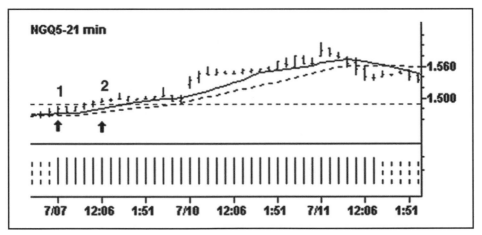

Figure 7–8 NGQ5 Timing Chart: Exit and Reverse

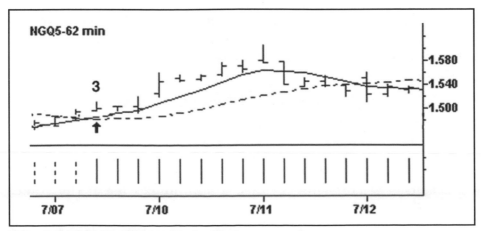

Figure 7–9 NGQ5 New Entry on Monitor Chart

trader is to be out of half his short position and in on half his long position, or flat.

At point 2, at 12:06 p.m the 12:00 noon cut-off has passed and prices have risen above the halfway point of the solid Harami line (above $1.491). The trader would now take profit on the second half of the short trade so that he would be net long on 50 percent of a new position.

At point 3 (in Figure 7–9), a long signal was generated on the monitor chart at 1:06 p.m. at $1.50. A check of the tick chart revealed that there was no opportunity to enter the market at a better level, so a stop was placed and executed at slightly above the trigger point ($1.501) on the second half of the position.

The average price of contracts purchased was $1.488 at this point, so the short trade had generated profits of $1.875 minus $1.488 to equal 0.387, or $3,870 per contract, minus slippage and commissions. Assuming slippage and commissions to be $100 and a typical trade of 250 contracts, the profit would be $942,500.

Subsequently, the market enjoyed a small rally, since the bear market was well established and the movement on the chart was simply corrective. Point 1 on the 21-minute chart in Figure 7–10 is the close of July 10 at a low of $1.491.

The close represents the end of a wave *b* of an *abc* three-wave correction. Based on the equal-to rules (see Chapter 3), a trader could expect the market to move somewhere between $1.56 to $1.604, where $1.56 would be the high if wave *c* is equal to wave *a*:

$$\$1.56 = \$1.491 + (1.52 - 1.45)$$

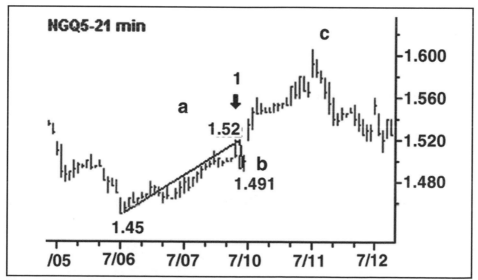

Figure 7–10 NGQ5 Projecting an *abc* Correction

Based on the longer-than rule, $1.604 is the high, if wave c is 62 percent greater than wave a:

$$\$1.604 = \$1.491 + 1.618(1.52 - 1.45)$$

Once the market breaches $1.56, the trader can begin to monitor for market turns.

At 10:21 a.m., on July 11, the market reached a high of $1.605, just one tick above the "longer" target. This was coincident at 11:24 a.m. with a confirmed divergence at a price of $1.565. According to exit rule 2, half the profit on the long trade is to be taken at this point.

Upon the generation of a short signal at point 3, Figure 7–11, the other half can be taken at 12:48 p.m. of the same day and 50 percent of the short trade can be entered at a price of approximately $1.545.

The trader now is to look either for confirmation on the monitor chart or a pullback and new signal on the timing chart. The pullback and new signal appeared on the timing chart on July 13 at 10:42 a.m. at a price of $1.50 (Figure 7–11, point 4). This occurred before confirmation appeared on the monitor chart. At this point, the second half of the short trade is to be added. (If the

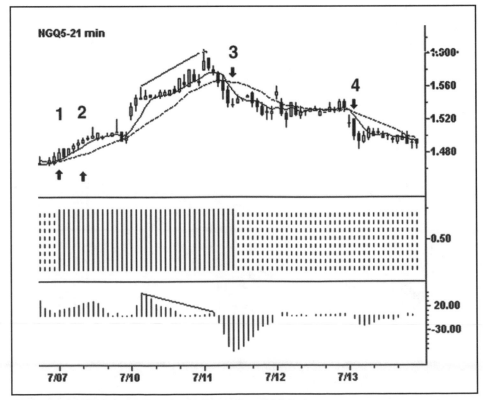

Figure 7–11 NGQ5 Longs Exited and Shorts Re-established

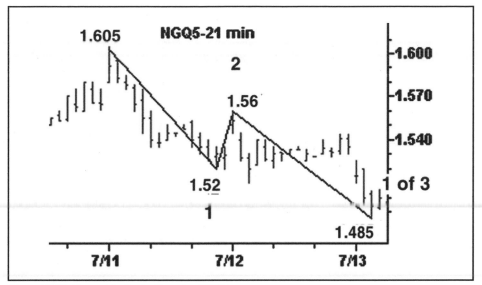

Figure 7–12 Downside Projections for NGQ5

trader had waited for confirmation on the monitor chart, he would not have entered the trade until July 19. However, because the market went into a sideways stall, the entry point on the monitor chart would have been at practically the same price as the timing chart.)

The small profit on the short-term long trade is $1.565 minus $1.488 to equal $0.077, or $770 per trade. Assuming $100 commission cost and slippage and a 250 contract trade size, a $167,500 profit is realized.

With a fully intact short trade as of the morning of the 13th, the potential for prices to fall can now be calculated. For the sake of evaluation, we will assume that the market has completed Waves 1 and 2 and the first smaller wave component of Wave 3. Wave 1 is the movement from $1.605 to $1.52 and Wave 1 of 3 is the movement from $1.56 to $1.485 (labeled 1 of 3 in Figure 7–12).

Wave One projects to about $1.36 for the entire move:

$$e^{[\ln 1.605 \,+\, 3(\ln 1.52 \,-\, \ln 1.605)]} \;=\; \$1.36;$$

Wave One of three projects to $1.35 for the entire Wave Three:

$$e^{[\ln 1.56 \,+\, 3(\ln 1.485 \,-\, \ln 1.56)]} \;=\; \$1.35; \text{ and}$$

to $1.37 for the end of the current wave:

$$\$1.495 \,+\, 1.618(1.485 \,-\, 1.56) \;=\; \$1.37.$$

There was a good probability of breaking $1.40 and perhaps going into the low $1.30s or lower. With an extension, prices could have fallen as low as $1.27:

$$e^{[\ln 1.605 \, + \, 3(\ln 1.485 \, - \, \ln 1.605)]} = \$1.27.$$

The market moved down and closed at $1.385, generating an extremely profitable trade. Staying short into the expiration, the profit from this trade would have been:

$1.544 (the average of exits and re-entries above) minus $1.385 to equal $0.159, or $1,590 per contract. Assuming a trade size of 250 contracts and $100 per round turn commission and slippage, a profit of $372,500 would have been made.

To review, the trader first shorted the market at $1.875. The short trade was held to a reversal point at $1.484. The resulting long trade was held to $1.565. The trader reshorted at $1.5225 and held the short to $1.385.

The net result was:

$1.875 − $1.488 = 0.387 − 0.01 (commission and slippage) =
0.377

$1.565 − $1.488 = 0.077 − 0.01 = 0.067

$1.5225 − $1.385 = 0.1375 − 0.01 = 0.1275

This represents a total gain of .5715 on this 2/3 and a net overall gain of $1.43 million on the overall strategy.

Example Two: July 1995

In this next example, a trade in the July 1995 COMEX silver contract is examined.

The trader should begin the evaluation by studying the daily chart (see Figure 7–13). In early March, the market begins to generate PeakOut set-up signals. At point 1, on the March 3 candlestick chart, a hammer pattern forms. This pattern is also supportive of a market turn.

While the PeakOscillator has generated a signal that is supportive of a market turn (confirming the morning star set-up), all three traditional indicators—the Stochastic, RSI, and MACD—failed entirely to register divergence. In addition, the hammer and two previous bars form a morning star set-up. This is a prime time to check the weekly chart, which shows a PeakOut set-up at point 1 (see Figure 7–14).

At this time, the shorter term charts are to be examined for confirming signals and for timing into a new trade, as indicated.

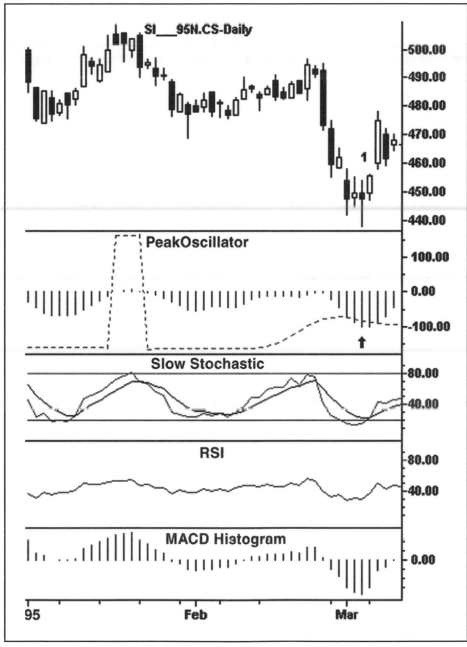

Figure 7–13 July 1995 Silver Daily Chart

A look at the hourly chart (see Figure 7–15), which in this case is the monitor chart, shows clear PeakOscillator divergence. At this point, the KaseCD has already crossed above the zero line.

At the open of business on the following day, March 6, the 20-minute timing chart (Figure 7–16) may be followed to time entry into the market.

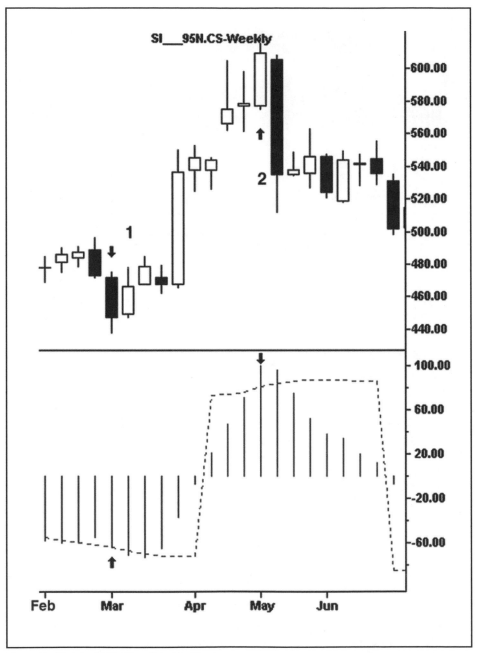

Figure 7–14 July 1995 Silver Weekly Chart

By analyzing the intraday timing chart on the 6th, a trader will note that long trades have been permissioned for some time. This indicates permission to take all long timing signals. There is also a divergence on both the PeakOscillator and KaseCD, lending additional weight to the long signal. Thus, we are permissioned to go long on the first crossover of the fast moving average from

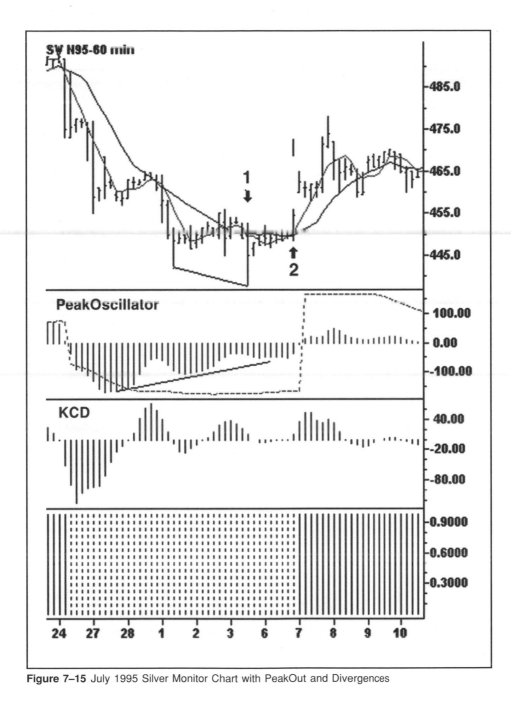

Figure 7–15 July 1995 Silver Monitor Chart with PeakOut and Divergences

below to above the slow moving average. This crossover takes place at 9:45 a.m. at a price of $4.48.

According to the rules, the second half of the trade should then be added either on a new cross to the upside of the short-term chart or a confirmed cross to the upside on the monitor chart.

On the short-term chart, the fast moving average remains above the slow for the remainder of the day, not generating new signals.

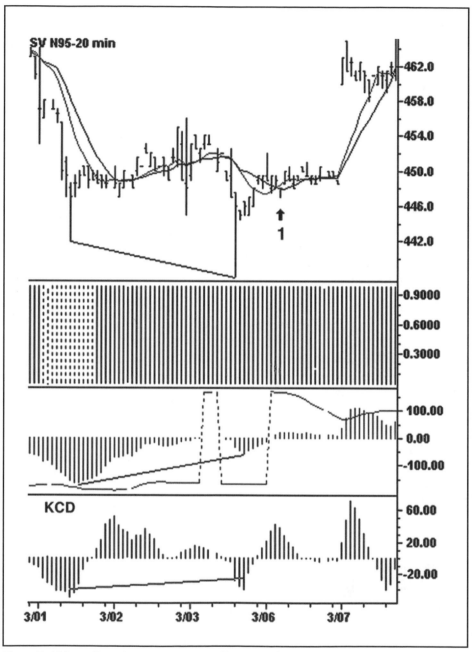

Figure 7–16 Long Entry Signal on July 1995 Silver Timing Chart

However, the monitor chart shows a crossover of the moving averages to the upside at point 2. The trade is then permissioned on the open the following morning, and upon completion of the first bar at 9:25 a.m.

The trader then drops down to the tick chart (see Figure 7–17) to fine-tune the entry. Looking at the market at around 9:45 a.m., there is a divergence on the Stochastic and there has been a minor down move since about 8:45 a.m. According to the fine-tune method (see Chapter 4), stops should be moved down to the intermediate peaks. The final stop should be placed at the intermediate peak, point 2, since this is the final intermediate peak before the turn. Thus, the trade would be filled upon a break of that stop level, which occurs at $4.61.

At this point, the trade may be followed on the monitor chart until confirmation is received on the daily chart. This confirmation comes on March 14, as shown on point 2 on the daily chart in Figure 7–18.

One hundred percent of this position is now held to the point at which the daily bar exhibits PeakOut set-ups, confirmed by the KaseCD divergence at point 3.

At point 3, where there are signs of a market turn (including KCD divergence, a PeakOut set-up, and evening star set-ups), defensive measures should be taken by raising stops to Dev-Stop

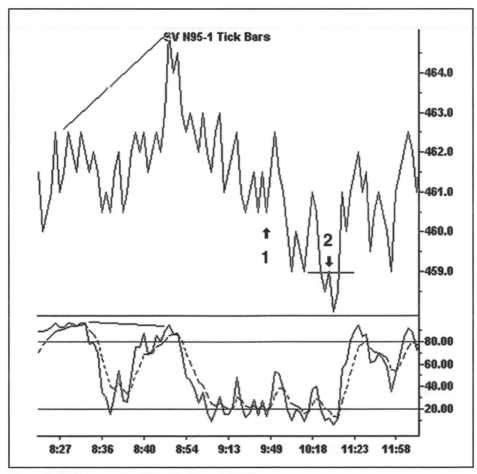

Figure 7–17 Entry on One-Tick July Silver 1995 Chart

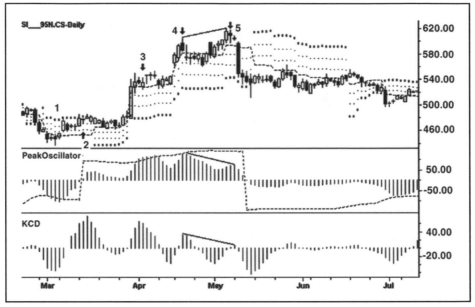

Figure 7–18 July 1995 Silver Daily Chart with Decision Points

one. (Two closes below the warning line is equivalent to breaking stop one.) The trader should also treat a morning star pattern confirmation as stop one.

Thus, at point 3, with a sign of a probable turn, the market should be evaluated more closely. Wave 1 indicates that even an extension longer than the move for Wave 3 would result in a price of only $5.39:

$$\$5.39 = \$4.625 + 1.618(4.85 - 4.38)$$

Wave 1 IX target calculation results in a price of $5.58:

$$\$5.58 = \$4.625 + .236(4.85 - 4.625),$$

which is consistent with the previous high of $5.50 and the ultimate high that is reached before the market turns at $5.53.

Waves 1, 2, and 3 of a 5-wave pattern have completed, where Wave 3 was highly extended (see Figure 7–19). In such cases, there are often shallow corrections, i.e., corrections smaller than 38 percent, usually in the 21 percent range. Indeed, the correction from the bottom of the move to the $5.53 level and back to the ultimate $5.26 low was 23.5 percent.

Looking at Wave 3, if Wave 5 is equal to Wave 3, it should project to about $6.17, or

$$\$6.17 = \$5.26 + (5.53 - 4.625).$$

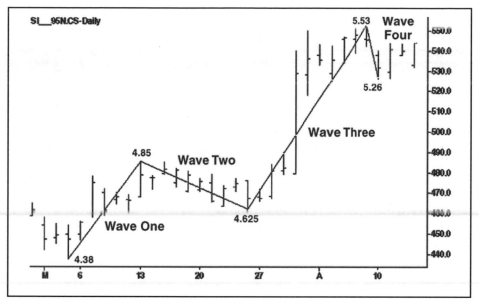

Figure 7–19 Daily Chart Wave Count

This expectation supports an expectation of both a moderate correction and a resumption back to the upside.

Following point 3, what appears to be a measuring gap occurs (see Chapter 6 Appendix, "Gaps"). The projection of the measuring gap is $6.45, calculated by taking the difference between the bottom of the gap, $5.45, minus the beginning of Wave 3 at $4.626. This equals 0.825, which is added to the top of the gap, $5.625.

$$\text{Measuring Gap Projection} = \$5.625 + .825 = \$6.45.$$

This is also consistent with the corrective extension for Wave 3, which projects to $6.40 as a completion of the move:

$$\$6.40 = 5.26 + 4.236(5.53 - 5.26).$$

The end of the move should occur somewhere in the $6.15 to $6.40 range.

At point 4 (see Figure 7–18), a clean PeakOut set-up is indicated and is much cleaner than the previous set-up. It also confirms the KaseCD. In addition, there is a dark cloud cover formation that failed to close below the midpoint. At this point, should the market close below this point the following day (somewhere in the vicinity of $5.842), half the profit should be taken.

At point 4, a dilemma exists because we are only part way between the smaller than and equal to targets for Wave 5. The target range has not been reached, but the market has exceeded the minimum distance for Wave 5, i.e., Wave 5 is already greater than 62

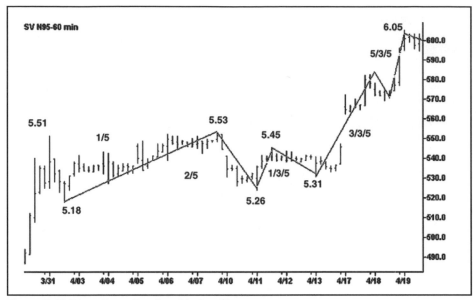

Figure 7–20 Wave Count Detail on Monitor Chart

percent of Wave 3 (which would have had Wave 5 culminating at a price of $5.82).

Also, looking at Wave 1, a normal move without an extended Wave 3 would be expected to reach about $5.95:

$$\$5.95 \; = \; e^{[\ln 4.38 \; + \; 3(\ln 4.85 \; - \; \ln 4.38)]}$$

The trader should now use a more detailed chart, in this case the 60-minute chart (see Figure 7–20) to evaluate the wave counts more closely. It appears that the end of Wave 3 was actually at $5.51, not $5.53. This difference of less than one-third of one percent does not change our overall targets much, but still means we must fine-tune our forecast.

Wave 5 actually began prior to the gap at $5.18 (the low following the $5.51 level), with $5.18 to $5.53 delineating Wave 1 of 5, and $5.53 to $5.26 delineating Wave 2 of 5. The length of Wave 1 of 5 formation projects to a completed Wave 5 at $6.30, using the Rule of Three is:

$$\$6.30 \; = \; e^{[\ln 5.18 \; + \; 3(\ln 5.53 \; - \; \ln 5.18)]}$$

The $5.26, $5.45, $5.31 points on Figure 7–20 appear to form Wave 1 of 3, according to the Elliott Wave Rules (see Chapter 3). This wave, using the IX rule (if it is Wave 1 and it is extended), projects to $5.90:

IX Projection = $5.90 = $5.31 + 4.236($5.45 − $ 5.31).

The end of Wave 3 at $6.05 is consistent with other evaluations. At this point, an estimate for Wave 4 of 5 will likely commence, with the completion of Wave 5, still remaining thereafter.

Once Waves 3 and 4 of 5 are complete, the shorter than rule for Wave 5 (62 percent of Wave 3) projects to $6.15 and the equal to rule projects to $6.46, again consistent with earlier forecasts. The corrective target is $6.30, in the middle of these two levels.

In light of this forecast and market view, the exit strategy should be considered with extra care. Wave 4 corrections can be deep and erratic. If we take a contra-trend trade, and then if the market turns back up after a corrective phase, the trader should exit the trade according to plan and reinstate a strategy in the direction of the trend.

On first bar of the 20th in Figure 7–22, a permission short signal is generated, following a gap to the downside, point 1. In accordance with the rules, since a gap precedes the signal, no other exit criteria must be met. The tick chart should be analyzed to time into the first leg of the short trade and exit 50 percent of the long position to spread risk by entering the trades in two halves.

Using the technique of moving the entry point up from higher lows to higher lows, the trade is finally entered at approximately $5.90.

According to the rules, 50 percent of the trade position can be executed on the second signal on the timing chart after a first permission signal on the monitor chart for the second half of the trade.

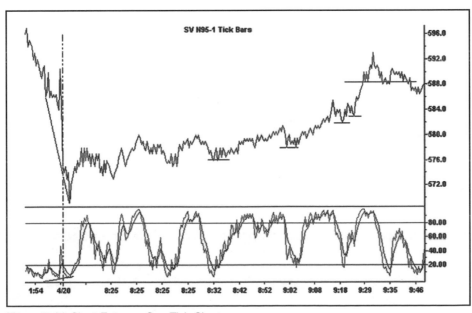

Figure 7–21 Short Entry on One-Tick Chart

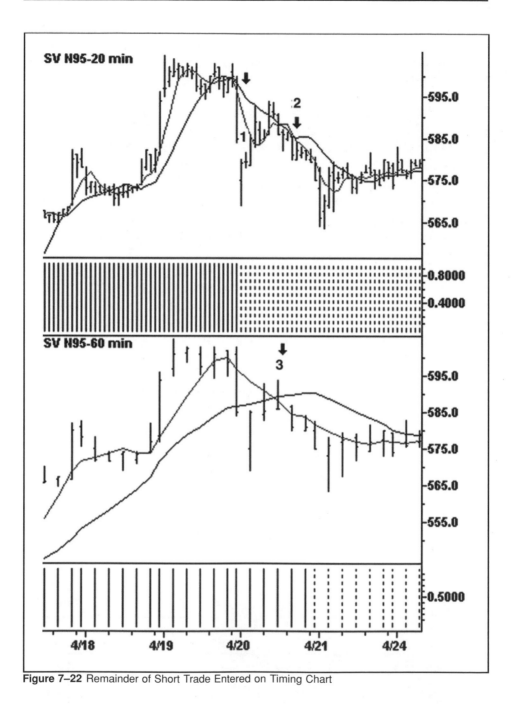

Figure 7–22 Remainder of Short Trade Entered on Timing Chart

The second permissioned signal on the timing chart is taken at 11:45 a.m. at $5.86. Taking the average of the prices at which the trader reversed from long to short, the result is $5.88. (Point 3 indicates where the signal was generated, i.e., after point 2, on the monitor chart.) The profit on this trade is $5.88 minus $4.545 to equal $1.335 per troy ounce.

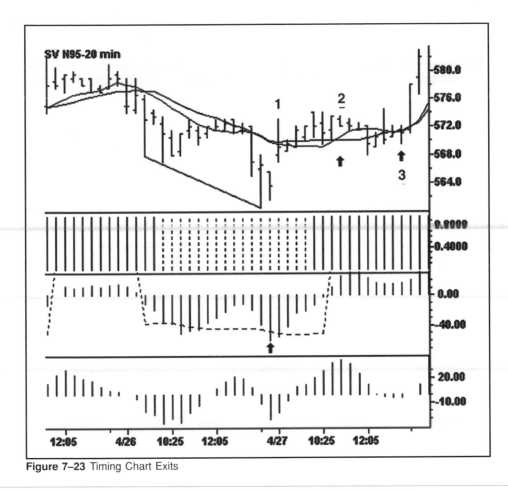

Figure 7–23 Timing Chart Exits

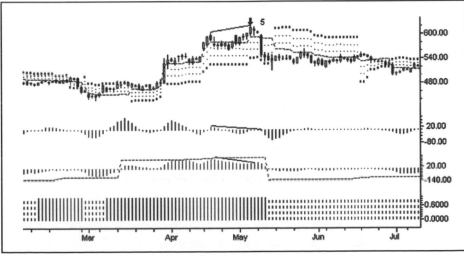

Figure 7–24 July 1995 Silver Daily

The first new long signal is generated at $5.72, for an average exit of $5.705 and first half entry at $5.72. The second half of the trade is entered on a second crossover at $5.71. Point 1 is at 8:45 a.m., point 2 is at 11:05 a.m., and point 3 is at 1:25 p.m. Thus, the re-entry into the long trade is at $5.715. The profit on the short-term short trade is $5.88 minus $5.705 to equal $0.175 per troy ounce.

The trade can be ridden down until a PeakOut is confirmed by divergence or other exit signals. Given that this is a countertrend trade, 50 percent of the trade is exited on the warning that the market may turn, thus, exiting 50 percent of the trade at $5.69.

At this point, a check of the daily chart reveals permission for long trades has been in place for months. Now the trader can switch to monitoring this trade on the daily chart at will.

On May 5, at point 5, a Harami line and star are accompanied by a PeakOut with divergence set-up and a KaseCD divergence confirmation. The star is a hanging man. Price is also in the target range for the end of the move.

As in earlier portions of these examples, the exit strategy here is to take half the profit on the completion of the candlestick pattern and/or the divergence in the daily chart. This puts the trader out of half his trade at $6.08.

At 10:25 a.m. the following morning, a crossover on the timing chart and a confirmed monitor chart signal occur on the close at $6:05. These indicate the second half of the trade is to be exited. This gives an average exit price of $6.065. The profit on the last leg of this trade is $6.065 minus $5.715 to equal $0.35 per troy ounce.

Thus, the reader can see that a multiple time frame trading system, using statistical indicators to identify market turns, as well as good stopping points, allows the trader not only to enter good trending markets early and effectively, but also to profit from shorter-term reversals in that trend.

In sum, the trader first went long in the market at $4.545 and then reversed to a short position at $5.88, and covered the short at $5.705. The trader went long once again at $5.715 and sold at $6.065.

The net result was:

$$\$5.88 - \$4.545 = \$1.335$$

$$\$5.88 - \$5.705 = \$0.175$$

$$\$6.065 - \$5.715 = \$0.35$$

The total gain was $1.86. On a one contract basis (5,000 troy ounce contract) this represents a gross of $9,300.00. Allowing $100.00 round turn for commissions and slippage reduces this to an even $9,000.00 net. If 250 contracts are involved, the net profit would be $2,250,000.00.

CHAPTER 8

Freedom from Time and Space with Universal Bars

The 15th edition of Albert Einstein's *Relativity, the Special and General Theory* includes an addendum called "Relativity and the Problem of Space." In it, Einstein maintains that our conceptions of time and space derive from our own human experience, the frame of reference that results from our empirical observations. This frame of reference is highly subjective. Our perceptions are limited to those dimensions we can easily comprehend using the five senses with which we examine the world. We should not make the assumption that, because these dimensions are all we can grasp conceptually, they are all that exist. If we could not see it, the grass would still be green. Our universe is both infinite and limited. Freeing our minds from preconceived notions of reality allows us to grasp larger concepts. We live in an infinite universe that is limited only by our own perceptions of it. Einstein encouraged us to free our minds, in this way hoping to arrive at a closer approximation of the truth. This ability to imagine concepts beyond our perceived reality is what has made mankind's intellectual progress possible.

We perceive the markets two-dimensionally, in terms of time and space (or, more accurately, time and volume), but we need to broaden our view. Volatility is proportional to the square root of time and of volume. When we look at price change or volatility relative to time or volume, we are looking at only one dimension of these variables. For a proportional relationship, we must square volatility.

While some recent innovations in the display of data have been developed, e.g., the introduction of tick volume bars, these bars have the same flaw. Change in price relative to tick volume is proportional to the square root of tick volume. Tick volume bars are superior to time bars in that they are less widely distributed. The ramification is that it is generally about 15 percent less risky, everything else being equal, to trade tick-volume bars.

It has been said that "removing the faults in a stagecoach may produce a perfect stagecoach, but it is unlikely to produce the first motor car." Thus, while traders improve their approaches by using both time bars and tick volume bars, we still basically just have a better stagecoach. If we want to achieve motor car status, we need to look at market activity relative to itself. We want to level the volatility playing field and in essence have absolute volatility constant with a near zero variance, with only the sign of the volatility (up or down, plus or minus) changes. Thus, we want to look at volatility with only one variable, not two—in a sense, to see it in the same dimension. As long as we look at time in relation to volume only, we are still limited by this square root (stagecoach) relationship.

The true range is directly proportional to volatility; it is proportional to the square root of time and also to the square root of tick volume, as is volatility. It only makes sense, given that we can now via the computer, easily look at the market according to true range, to do so. There are, of course, point and figure charts that display pure market activity. However, point and figure charts do not lend themselves to most traditional indicator methods. Thus, the introduction of Kase Universal Bars, equal range bars, where the range is set by specific criteria.

RULES FOR FORMATTING EQUAL RANGE BARS

Some rules for the minimum range, at which it is reasonable to view the market, as well as a rule or two about the maximum range, must be established. True range can be used on an intraday basis to clarify market direction.

The criteria for the minimum-size true range is that the minimum must be three times the tick volatility. This is the same criteria discussed in Chapter 4 relative to setting up charts. Tick volatility equals the average difference between ticks. This is, in a sense, the smallest price move possible in the market, the minimum delta price. Without a multiple of at least one price change, bars will not make sense. Bars must have a certain amount of minimum activity to be meaningful. Therefore, we use three times the minimum or average tick change as the minimum at which we will look at the market. If we wish to see the market in any further detail, we must use a tick chart.

For markets that have an open and a close, i.e., that do not trade on a 24-hour basis, there is an upside or largest bar rule. On the upside, the true range is equivalent to the average range of the day, divided by the square root of two, since the minimum intraday bar looked at is a half-day. For markets that do not have an open and a close, this artificial higher limitation does not apply. For these, the equivalent of a day can be considered as 24 hours. We then take the average range (the 24-hour period) and form bars of equal range, where the range is equal to the average 24-hour range. Then we can scale up and down in range, according to the square-root of the multiple. For example, for a monitor chart with a 1/5 of a day bar, we divide the 24-hour range by the square root of five to get this bar's target range.

Once the rules are established, we simply read in the ticks, calculate the true range, and stop the bar when we meet the true range. We also have rules for times when we exceed the true range and when we do not make the true range. These are necessary because the market tick may put us outside our target and we cannot adjust a bar any closer, preventing further adjustments to the bar, for example, if we set a range to $0.10, some $0.11 bars, some $0.12 bars, etc. We are getting as close to looking at the market in a pure sense as we possibly can, and are purifying our data to look at it in a truer sense.

The true range can be used as a proxy for rate of change or logarithmic growth. Generally speaking, we use this technique on an intraday basis. Thus, most of the time, we will be looking at market moves in which we can discount the curvature of the market.

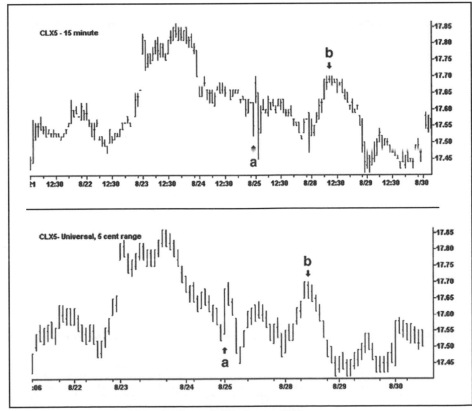

Figure 8–1 Time versus Universal Bars, CLX5, August 1995

To see the difference between universal and normal time bars, we will examine the November, 1995 West Texas Intermediate crude oil contract (see Figure 8–1). We have selected a 15-minute bar for our study, which, over the month evaluated (8/22–9/21/95), had an average true range of five cents. We compared these average five cent range bars with universal bars, targeted to format themselves to a five cent range.

We found that the amount by which the actual range of the 15-minute bars differed from the five-cent average range was by three cents, exhibiting a standard deviation of 2.2. The universal bars differed from the five cent average by 0.7 cents and had a standard deviation of 0.5. Thus, there is about a 75 percent reduction in the variability of the bars. Considering that this reduction also encompasses overnight gaps that cannot be removed, this is significant.

The first set of charts shows the data in the earlier part of our month, around August 22 through 28. We see at first glance that the Kase Universal bars are regular and close in size. The 15-minute bars are highly erratic, some of the bars having a high-

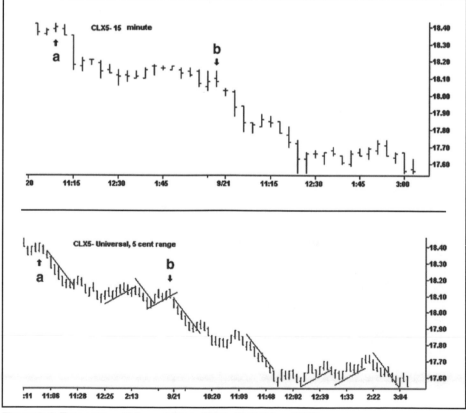

Figure 8–2 Time versus Universal Bars, CLX5, September 1995

low range of zero and others having a wide range. In the case of the Kase Universal bars, where the bars are larger than normal (e.g., bar *a*), in Figure 8–1, this is because the difference in ticks was such that a five-cent bar was impossible to format, i.e., the difference between one tick and the next was greater than five cents.

The regularity and clean turn to the down move at point b can be noted on the Kase Universal bars, as opposed to the choppy turn on the 15-minute bars.

Market activity picked up considerably on September 20 and 21, illustrated by the larger number of bars in the universal bars generated on these days. Of course, the 15-minute bar chart simply generates the same number of bars everyday regardless of volatility. The turns to the downside are clearer at points a and b and at the support and resistance lines formed on the Kase Universal bars. All the support and resistance lines were drawn at exactly the same angle to show how clearly and closely the Kase Universal bars tend to hold certain angles on market moves.

This is a new technique and, as such, presently is in an experimental stage.

Our observations to date are that momentum and other sensitive techniques work well with these bars, and, thus, trading can be sped up without degrading performance. We note, however, that timing into the market is better done with sensitive indicators, e.g., the MACD or Stochastic % K versus %D crossovers, rather than by moving averages or other trending techniques. The reason appears to be that the turns in the universal bars are so clean and sharp that the lag in moving averages and other trending techniques is exaggerated, as it always is in V-type turns.

Thus, we expect that a major improvement of the universal bars, in addition to reducing risk, will be to clean up and clarify market turns and allow traders to use more aggressive timing techniques without sacrificing trading accuracy.

REFERENCES

Poulos, E. Michael [1992]. "Do Persistent Cycles Exist?" *Technical Analysis of Stocks & Comodities*, Volume 10:September.

[1002]. "Futures According to Trend Tendency," *Technical Analysis of Stocks & Commodities*, Volume 10:January.

[1991]. "Of Trends and Random Walks," *Technical Analysis of Stocks & Commodities*, Volume 9:February.

Saitta, Alex [1995]. "Trending on a Historical Basis," *Technical Analysis of Stocks & Commodities*, Volume 13:August.

INDEX

Appel, George, xii

Bars
  equal range bars, 140
  numbering protocol, 54
  synthetic bars, 585-56,57
  universal bars, Chapter 8
  upside (largest) bar rule, 140
Bell curve (normal distribution) 17
Black box systems, 6
Blunt instrument systems, 2, 4, 5
Bookstaber, Richard, 94

Candlestick charts, 47, 97-103, 114-
    116, 120, 121, 126-128, 132,
    137, 138
Candlestick patterns, 97-103
Chart formations, 40-47
  continuation patterns, 46, 47
    flags, 46
    measuring gaps, 46-49
    pennants, 46
    wedges, 46
  reversal patterns, 40-46
    coils (springs), 45,46
    double tops/bottoms, 41
    head and shoulders, 41-44
    island reversal, 40
    spike tops/V bottoms, 40
    symmetrical triangle, 44-45
Computers, xiii, 1
Continuation patterns,
    See Chart formations

Dev-Stop, See Kase Adaptive
    Dev-Stop, Chapter 6
Directional Movement indicator
    (DMI), xii
Donchian, Richard, 5, 48
Diversification
  portfolio trading, 48
  time, Chapter 4, See also Chapter
    7 examples

Elliott Wave Theory, 8, 26-28, 29-40,
    125, 132-134
  forecasting grid, 38-40
  rule of three, 29, 31, 32, 35-36
    equal to rule, 33-34, 123
    longer than rule, 34, 124
    shorter than rule, 31-33
Entries, fine tuning, 69
Equal range bars, 140
Exit strategies, Chapter 6, See also
    Kase Adaptive Dev-Stops
  candlestick to accelerate exits,
    97-103, 114-116,120, 121,
    123
  divergence, 75, 78, 83, 87, 102,
    111, 116, 138
  fear, 92
  market turns, Chapter 5
  noise, 92-96
  overbought/oversold, 78
  profit taking, 83, 87, 113, 133
  risk, 92-96
  volatility, 92-96
    true range as proxy, 93, 94
  warning signals, 113

Exponential Moving Average, xvi
Extensions, 29

Fibonacci, 10, 26
Fine tuning, *See Time*
  Diversification
Forecasting, Chapter 3
Forecasting Grid, *See Elliott Wave*
  Theory
Fundamental analysis, 24

Gaps, 106-110
  common gap, 106, 107
  breakaway gap, 96, 106, 108, 110
  exhaustion gap, 108, 109
  measuring gap, 46-47, 106, 107

Head and Shoulders, *See Chart*
  formations

Indicators
  automatically adaptive, 2-3
  trending, 52
Island Reversal, 40, *See also*
  Reversal patterns

Kase Adaptive Dev-Stop, Chapter 6,
  113, 118, 119, 131, *See also Exit*
  Strategies
  charting, 97
  three level stop, 96

KaseCD
  definition, 83
  with Kase PeakOscillator,
    74, 83-87, 111, 116, 117,
    127-129, 131-133, 138
Kase PeakOscillator, 74, 77-87,
  89, 90, 102-105, 111,
  115-121, 126, 128-133, 137, 138,
  See also Exit Strategies
Kase Permission Stochastic, 55-56,
  58-63
Kase Universal Bars, Chapter 8

MACD, xii, 75, 79, 82-84, 85, 126,
  127, 143
Malthus, Robert, 4
Markov processes, 87
Market turns, Chapter 5
Markets
  behavioral activity, 4
  corporate trading, 4
  forecasting, Chapter 3, *See also*
    Chart Formations, Elliott
    Wave, Fibonacci
  forecasting laws, 21-25
  grid, 38-40
  geometry, 25-26
  overbought/oversold,
    59-62, 75-77
  predictability, 9
  psychology, 4, 9
  symmetry across time frames, 7
Momentum, 74, 75
Momentum filters, 53
Momentum indicators, *See KaseCD,*
  Kase PeakOscillator, Moving
  Averages, MACD, RSI,
  Stochastic
Monitor chart,
  See Time Diversification
Monte Carlo simulations, 88, 89
Moving Average indicator, xv, xvi,
  50, 51, 53, 63, 122, 129, 136
Moving Average Convergence
  Divergence indicator, *See*
  MACD

Normal distribution, 17-18
Normalized indicators, 76

Optimization, 2
Oscillator, *See also Kase*
  PeakOscillator
  normalized, 76
  simple, 76

Outliers, xvi, 10, 12-13, 95
Overbought/Oversold, 59-62, 75-77

Parabolic indicator, xii
Pareto's Law, 1-2
PeakOscillator, *See Kase PeakOscillator*
Permission screens
    Kase PeakOscillator, 112, 117, 118, 120, 129
    Kase Permissioned Stochastic, 60, 61
    moving average, 120, 124, 128, 130, 136, 137
Poulous, Mike, 88
Psychology
    human behavior, 4
    mass psychology, 8, 9

Random Walk Index, 88-90
Relative Strength Index, *See RSI*
Retracements, 30, 36, 37
Reversal patterns, 40-46
    coils (or springs), 45-46
    head and shoulders, 41-44
    island reversal, 40
    symmetrical triangle, 44-45
Rolling week, v, 55-56
RSI, xii, 75, 76, 80, 126, 127
Rule of 3, *See Elliott Wave Theory*
RWI, *See Random Walk Index*

Saitta, Alex, 88
Scaling, *See Time Diversification*
Screening trades, 49
    permissioning, 50-53
    momentum filters, 53
    trending filters, 50-53
Statistics
    cumulative distribution, 18
    dependent variable, 19
    histogram, 17
    independent variable, 19
    mean, 12, 94
    median, 13
    Monte Carlo simulations, 88
    normal distribution, (bell curve), 17-18

range, 13, 14. *See also True Range*
    skew distributions, 19, 96
    standard deviation, 16, 95
    stem and leaf (stemplot), 16
    stochastic processes, 77, 87
    variance, 14, 95-96
Stochastic, xii, 53, 55-56, 58-60, 63, 72-73, 75, 79, 81, 115, 116, 118, 119, 126, 127, 130, 131, 143
Stochastic processes, 77, 87
Stops, *See Exit strategies*
Synthetic bars, 55-57

Technical analysis, 24
Testing, 76, 77
Time diversification, Chapter 4
    fine tuning, 69, 118, 130, 131, 134
    monitor chart, 55, 64-66, 111-113, 116, 117, 122-125, 129, 131, 134-136, 140
    permissioned trading, 50-52
    scaling, 49, 63-69
    screening time frame, 55, 111, 112
    screening trades, 49
    timing chart, 64, 65, 67, 117, 122-124, 128, 137
Trending filters, 49-53
True range, 69-71, 93, 94, 95, 140-142

Universal bars, Chapter 8

Volatility, 93-96, 139 140
    expansions, 96
    skew, 95, 96
    variance, 95

Whipsaws, 52, 53, 58, 59
Wilder, Wells, xii, 94
Williams, Larry, 96

ORDERING INFORMATION

Readers interested in receiving more information about Kase and Company, Inc., or those who would like a software trial of the Kase indicator and support systems, may contact Kase directly at (505)-237-1600, Suite C, 1000 Eubank Blvd., Albuquerque, NM 87112, or by facsimile at (505)-237-1659, or through Irwin Professional Publishers, 1333 Burr Ridge Parkway, Burr Ridge, IL 60521, (708)-789-6933.

A trial of the indicators is not included in this book because technological advances and updates of indicators occur so rapidly that the software package could become obsolete before the book purchase date. Kase wants to ensure that readers have the most recent edition of their indicators. Additionally, it is important that the software be compatible with the users' charting systems.

Thus, Kase asks orderers to include the following information with their requests:

1. Data services used or charting services owned or used.
2. Category of trader:
   a. Full-time private trader
   b. Fund manager
   c. Corporate or institutional trader
   d. Corporate risk manager
   e. Broker
   f. Private investor, employed in other field
   g. Other _____
3. Company name.
4. Type of computer, and amount of RAM.